Mrs Webb
SOU

D1395249

THE LAST HORSEMEN

A century ago, power on farms was provided by one and a half million heavy horses. Today, heavy horses are almost a thing of the past, except for one place: Sillywrea Farm in Northumberland, where John Dodd's family have lived for more than 150 years. This is the last farm in the country where all the work is done by horses. Together with his son-in-law David Wise and five huge Clydesdales, John runs his farm to the rhythms of the seasons, and although the work is hard, the pace is unhurried as John and David work through the year.

THE LAST HORSEMEN

THE LAST HORSEMEN

by

Charles Bowden

WANDSWORTH PUBLIC LIBRARIES

Magna Large Print Books
Long Preston, North Yorkshire,
BD23 4ND, England.

British Library Cataloguing in Publication Data.

Bowden, Charles   5 0 0 9 8 2 2 6 2
     The last horsemen.

     A catalogue record of this book is
     available from the British Library

     ISBN   0-7505-2158-9

First published in Great Britain 2001 by Granada Media,
an imprint of André Deutsch Limited

Text Copyright © Charles Bowden 2001

Photographs ©   Mike Caldwell, Tony Stone, Lee Sutterby, John
Dodd's personal collection, Beamish North of England Open Air
Museum, The Bowes Museum, Newcastle Journal, Tyne Tees
Television, Hunter Adair, Allan Potts, Simon Crouch, Go-Britain
Ltd and Charles Bowden

Cover illustration © Lee Sutterby and Mike Caldwell
by arrangement with Granada Media

The right of Charles Bowden to be identified as the author of
this work has been asserted by him in accordance with the
Copyright, Designs and Patents Act, 1988

Published in Large Print 2003 by arrangement with
André Deutsch Limited

All Rights reserved. No part of this publication may be
reproduced, stored in a retrieval system, or transmitted in any
form or by any means, electronic, mechanical, photocopying,
recording or otherwise without the prior permission of the
Copyright owner.

Magna Large Print is an imprint of Library Magna Books Ltd.
Printed and bound in Great Britain by
T.J. (International) Ltd., Cornwall, PL28 8RW

Acknowledgements

First and foremost I would like to thank John and Maggie Dodd and David, Frances and Richard Wise for granting me the privilege of filming their unique way of farming – and for providing me with so much information for this book. They have always made me welcome at Sillywrea, and I count myself lucky to have made a record of life at a very special farm, one where heavy horses still reign supreme.

Many people enjoyed the television series *The Last Horsemen* which my company shot over three years at Sillywrea. My thanks go to the cameramen I work with: Simon Crouch, Lee Sutterby and Kip Halsey, and to the staff of Imagine in Newcastle, including film editor David Hindmarsh and sound mixer Andy Ludbrook. John Cook also composed a beautiful theme tune.

I pay tribute to Northern Arts, who helped me to kick-start the film project with a small grant from their Northern Production Fund. And I'm grateful to Graeme Thompson and Jane Bolesworth at Tyne Tees Television for commissioning the television series and encouraging the book which grew out of it.

The enthusiasm shown by Susanna Wadeson at Granada Media and Nicky Paris at André Deutsch was greatly instrumental in getting the book off the ground, and my editor Gillian Holmes at André Deutsch was a model of calm professionalism in her handling of the project.

I'm also indebted to the following: Hunter Adair, for his advice about Clydesdale horses; Peter Burgon, for his research into farm workers' conditions in the 1920s; and the Rev. David Perkins, for background into Methodist history in the north of England.

A particular thank you goes to my father, John Bowden, who worked as a farm labourer from 1926 to 1935 and then ran his own farm in Northumberland for the next 50 years. His crystal-clear memories of farm life before the war were a constant source of inspiration for this book.

Last but not least, I thank my wife Elspeth for the support and encouragement she continually gives me.

Contents

Extract from *Akenfield* by Ronald Blyth, Allen Lane, The Penguin Press, 1969, reproduced by permission of David Higham Associates

Author's Note

In the hot summer of 1976 I was working as agricultural editor of the *Newcastle Journal* when I heard a rumour that there was a farmer in Northumberland who was still using heavy horses on the land. It seemed unlikely, but I decided to check it out. When I finally tracked down John Dodd at Sillywrea Farm on a sunny July afternoon I was struck by a sight which was quite unique. Here was a man alone in the field, cutting grass with a reaper drawn by two lumbering Clydesdale horses. It was as though time had stood still. Changes which had swept through farming since the 1940s seemed to have bypassed this particular corner of the country.

John, a ruddy-faced, barrel-chested farmer with a twinkle in his eye, made me feel welcome. Haytime is an anxious season, but John seemed in no hurry. He got down from the reaper and, holding the horses' reins while they munched on the newly-mown grass, he told me his story. The article I wrote after that visit was entitled

11

'Horse Power'. It was the first time the outside world had caught up with a farm which time, it seemed, had forgotten.

Over the years I kept in touch with John. When, in 1986, I made a film for Tyne Tees Television about his friend, the elderly ploughman Tom Forster, I included a series of mini-dramas in costume, depicting incidents that had happened earlier in Tom's life. John kindly provided the horses for these – and even appeared in one scene, complete with makeup, pre-war clothes (his own striped collarless shirt and waistcoat) and a false moustache! If he felt awkward in this strange garb he didn't show it. He was happy to help out on a programme that honoured someone he respected.

In January 1998 I ran into John again after a gap of a few years. We'd both made our way to the church in the snowbound village of Cambo in Northumberland for the funeral of Tom Forster. The old ploughman had ploughed his last furrow and mourners had come from far and wide to bid him farewell. 'Aye,' said John, 'Old Tom will be missed. He was a great character.'

John's farm is called Sillywrea. This means 'Quiet Corner'. I asked him what the horses were up to these days in his quiet corner of the countryside. 'Oh,' he said. 'Usual winter jobs. Ploughing a bit of lea. Leading muck out from the byres.'

It sounded matter of fact. To John these may be routine jobs. But as I pictured them in my mind's eye I realised that no one else in the country would still be doing them. Certainly not with heavy horses and certainly not on a genuine working farm. I decided I must make a visual record of John's life before the countryside lost another great farming character.

The following week, cameraman Simon Crouch and I turned up to film the first scene, a farrier at work on the horses at Sillywrea. The project had begun.

For the next three years I returned to the farm many times, accompanied either by Simon or by two other cameramen, Lee Sutterby and Kip Halsey. We met John's wife Maggie, his daughter Frances, her husband David and their son Richard, along with Norman Barber, a retired lorry driver who grew up with horses and who now helps out at busy times. We recorded every event on the farm, every machine, every season. We filmed in detail how John and David broke in a young foal, Sandy – something which has rarely been seen on television. We accompanied the horsemen to farm sales and auction marts, and we were there when the family went to chapel and to their local New Year's Eve celebrations. The result was a priceless film archive of a way of life which has virtually vanished from the rest of Britain.

When I showed some of the material to Tyne Tees Television their reaction was immediate. They commissioned my company, CBTV, to make *The Last Horsemen*, six half-hour programmes which have since been shown on ITV. A video of the series followed.

In this book I describe the life of those Last Horsemen, two farmers who excel at rearing cattle and sheep, who choose to run their farm on a system which may seem outmoded to many but which works for them. Power is provided by their five Clydesdales: Jock, Dick, Davey, Sandy and Robin. Everything at Sillywrea stems from them. They are the pulsating heart of the farm. The seasons change but they remain constant, ever willing to work.

I've also tried to show that while they may be the last of the line, John and David have direct links – through their horses, their machines and the way they farm – to an agricultural world that has gone for ever but which stirs in many a strong sense of longing for the past. John says: 'They were hard times, but they were good times.' Is it reality, or is it myth? It's difficult to say. Some ancient farm labourers say they were treated like slaves in the early years of the 20th century. But there are many who would willingly turn back the clock to the days when the heavy horse prevailed.

Where do John and David fit into today's complex farming picture? In the sense that they produce beef and lamb, they are no different from other Northumberland live-stock farmers. Their industry has been beset by one crisis after another – falling profits, BSE, Foot and Mouth Disease – but they continue to plough their own furrow. So long as they can carry on making a living, they intend to stick to horses.

Elsewhere in Britain, there's been the odd instance of a farmer supplementing his income by hiring his heavy horses to breweries or for parades. Some have charged people for spending a weekend working with horses on the land. Others have tried forestry, working with their horses to pull logs out of the woods. But David and John show no desire to diversify.

Their life may have a gentle pace, but it is a full life all the same. On a farm like Silly-wrea, there's always work to be done. Much of it enjoyable work.

'If I had my life to live over again, I'd still work with the horses,' says John. 'It may be slow, but I get by in my own quiet way. I guess some people have looked strangely at me over the years, but it doesn't bother me if they smile and shake their heads. I don't criticise their type of farming.

'I like this way of life and the horses are part of it. It's an art to work a horse, something to be proud of. I've never been a salmon fisherman but it's like playing a fish. It's not strength that keeps the horses in check, not voice either. It's just the right touch on the reins.'

David is equally firm in his commitment to a life with horses. They may be far slower than tractors, which David used to drive. But because they're appreciably lighter than tractors they do much less damage to the land in winter, which seems to be a season that gets wetter every year. In their own unhurried, meticulous way the Horsemen get all the jobs done in the right season. The land does not suffer from being worked with horses. 'I will certainly try and continue to use horses myself,' David insists. 'And my wife Frances I know will support me in that. Hopefully our son Richard will too in later years, so long as farming remains viable.'

Farm & Family

Sillywrea

Thirty miles inland from where it flows into the North Sea, the River Tyne splits in two, one river pushing north towards the Scottish Border, the other heading west and south to its source in the Pennines. Cross the South Tyne by a handsome stone bridge and climb through woodlands to crest a ridge about 700 feet above sea level. All around, the landscape is typical of south-west Northumberland: stone walls slanting across meadows, open moorland in the far distance. But glance to your right and you'll see something which is certainly not typical of country life in the 21st century: heavy horses working in the fields.

Change happens slowly in this remote part of England. But even here farmers got rid of their horses and switched to tractors more than 50 years ago, following a trend which swept through the rest of the country after the outbreak of the Second World War. But not John Dodd. He stuck defiantly to his horses. At Sillywrea Farm all the work is still done by the five Clydesdales lovingly looked after by John and his son-in-law David Wise.

The two men are the last of a long line of horsemen.

A century ago power on farms was supplied by one and a half million heavy horses. They were the pride of rural Britain, and the men who worked with them were the elite among farm workers. The horsemen knew the secret of how to break in young horses and also how to get the best out of them on the land.

But today heavy horses are almost a thing of the past. True, they can be seen in all their glory at agricultural shows, decked in glistening harness and paraded round the main ring. They can be found in a handful of visitor centres which focus on agricultural history. And a dwindling number of breweries still use them to pull drays round city streets. But kept purely as a source of power on the land they're virtually extinct.

Five huge Clydesdale horses provide the pulling power at Sillywrea: Jock, Dick, Davey, Sandy and Robin. Between them they haul the machines which plough, sow and harvest the crops.

The farm's income is derived from cattle and sheep. But its activities revolve round the horses.

John Dodd's family have lived at Sillywrea for more than 150 years and for all that time horses have been a mainstay of the farm. John has loved horses since he was a child. He's worked on his farm since he was 15 and even now, at 72 and with one heart attack behind him, he has no plans to give up. Horses are his life.

His wife Maggie accepted that John was passionate about horses when she married him 47 years ago. 'When you marry the farmer, you marry the farm,' she says calmly. 'The horses have always been part of our life.'

David Wise is 47. He has been working side by side with his father-in-law since he married John's daughter Frances 13 years ago. He's vowed to keep on with the horses and hopes his 12-year-old son Richard will continue the family tradition.

Frances learned to handle horses when she joined her father on the farm at the age of 16. She continued to work with them until she married 15 years later. And while it's the men who do all the horse work now, Frances is closely involved in looking after the cattle and sheep, particularly at lambing time.

Life at Sillywrea has a slow, unhurried pace, but John and David don't see themselves as old-fashioned. They manage to get all the work done in the right season. Their farm produces good crops of hay, barley and turnips. Compared to modern farms the most noticeable difference is the silence. Instead of the harsh drone of a tractor, a pair of Clydesdales ploughing the land create a symphony of countryside sounds: the jingle of harness, the cry of the seagulls and the scrape of ploughshare on soil.

They are sounds of another age, but they live on at Sillywrea.

The Farm

Sillywrea, as I mentioned, means 'quiet corner'. The farm could not have a more fitting name. It lies in a hollow at the end of a lane which branches off a little-used country road. Sheltered by a clump of trees – chestnut, sycamore and beech – it has the remnants of an orchard, a small garden and a neat cluster of stone farm buildings.

There are records of a farm settlement at Sillywrea going back to the 16th century. The steading we see today originates mainly from

24

the 19th century, with its L-shaped layout and arched hemmels. It's typical of its period.

John's great grandfather bought the farm from Langley Baronry in 1848. The farm ledger of that year still exists. In faded lettering, he lists the animals he took with him when he moved to Sillywrea, including a nine-year-old black mare worth £29 and an 11-year-old black horse worth £16. A handful of cows provided income: the following year he went to market to sell three hundredweights of cheese at 22 shillings (£1.10) per hundredweight and seven firkins of butter at 39 shillings (£1.95) per firkin.

The farm's wet fields were drained (3,850 three-inch tiles at 25 shillings (£1.25) a thousand); the mole-catcher was paid ten shillings (50 pence) a year to get rid of moles; scrub was cleared from Clover Field at a cost of 12 shillings (60 pence) and a ploughman was taken on for six days at two shillings (ten pence) a day.

The farm was being knocked into shape by its new owner. To the eastern side of the farm buildings was a gin-gang, a conical, single-storey shed in which a horse walked round in a circle pulling a beam linked to a corn thresher. These machines were common in rural Britain at the time. For some reason, the gin-gang was pulled down. And on its site, in 1870, John's great grandfather built a new south-facing house, using stone from a quarry on his land.

Apart from a spacious timber-framed implement shed, put up by John and David in 1997, and a lean-to stock building roofed in corrugated iron which was erected by John in the 1960s, the buildings at Sillywrea haven't changed a great deal since they went up 150 years ago. As such, they contain much of interest.

One unusual feature is a sheep dipper built by John's grandfather around the end of the 19th century and one of the first of its kind in the district. Most dippers, then and now, are positioned out in the open next to sheep pens, but this one is inside a sheep shed. It's not used now, but in its day it certainly helped to streamline the farm's sheep dipping system.

In the winter, cattle at Sillywrea are housed in a series of small byres much as they were on many livestock farms in the years leading up to the Second World War. The muck they make is removed daily by horse and cart.

Hay and straw are stored in a big stone barn which has a large double door opening onto the cobbled farmyard and internal doors leading to the stable and cow-sheds.

The workshop, located under the granary in a corner of the stone barn, is the hub of the farm. It contains all the tools needed to keep the family's collection of horse-drawn implements in good running order, as well as a myriad of bits and pieces which might, in John words, 'come in handy one day'.

The workshop, too, has visible reminders of a practice which was once general. Nailed to the wooden beams are the colourful agricultural show prize tickets won by John's father in the 1930s and 1940s. Many are festooned with cobwebs and curling at the edges, but they give a glimpse of what used to be.

There's a series of prizes from the now defunct South Tyne Show held at Haltwhistle on 14 September 1946. George Dodd must have swept the board that year. Then there's evidence of a trip to Newcastleton Moor in July 1939, where a third prize was won at the Northumberland Agricultural Society's annual three-day show. There's a first prize at Slaley Show in 1938, tickets from Carlisle and Hexham fatstock shows, and much more.

Displays like this were often seen tacked to

the beams on livestock holdings run by men who were proud of their animals' prize-winning records. But with old buildings being swept away on many farms, another link with the past is disappearing and it's only in a few traditional places like Sillywrea that it lives on.

Sillywrea extends to 200 acres, of which 10 acres are barley, eight acres are in turnips and fodder beet, and 40 acres are cut for hay. The rest is grazed by the farm's 200 ewes and 30 cows and calves.

Over the last century, there has been a remorseless trend towards larger farm units. In 1875 there were 550,000 farms in England, Scotland and Wales. Today there are just over 200,000. 'At one time it was a nice living, 200 acres,' says John. 'But unfortunately farms are just getting bigger and bigger. People now reckon a 300-acre place is just a small place, and some say you need 1000 acres for a viable farm.

'I don't like the way things are going. To me, it's a vicious circle. The price of tractors and tractor-drawn machinery is so high these days that farmers seem to need more land to justify them. So they go out and borrow money to buy more land.

'I'm on the pension now and meant to be

retired, which is a good thing in a way. There's not enough land here to support two families. It's a great shame, because we were always brought up with the view that family farms were the backbone of England. But the way things seem to be going is very worrying.

'A farm where the farmhouse and buildings have been sold for development and where the land's been snapped up by neighbours, well, it'll never go back to being a family farm. It's lost for ever.'

John acknowledges that farmers are notorious for complaining about the state of their business. But he contends that today's farming crisis is every bit as bad as the farming slump in the 1930s. It could even be worse. 'My father used to say that when farming was in a depression between the two world wars, everything hit rock bottom. Prices were low for what you sold. And they were low for what you bought. What's different in the present day is that what we're selling has hit the bottom, but what we're buying in hasn't dropped.'

There's not much else that a farmer could do on Sillywrea apart from rearing stock. 'It's really a grass farm,' says John. 'When the family first came here in 1848 they ploughed a couple of fields and then sowed them back down to grass. Even in the First World War there wasn't any tillage. My grandfather offered the farm to the Ministry of Agriculture in 1914 on condition they put it back to the same state they found it, but they didn't take him up on it. He'd always said it wasn't suitable land for ploughing anyway, and to a certain extent he was right too.'

That's how things stayed until 1939. Then orders came to plough out some of the fields to provide more food for the country, and John has ploughed some of the land every year since then.

John Dodd

No whisper of lover, no trilling of bird
Can stir me as hooves of the horses have
   stirred.

                Will H. Ogilvie

John Dodd was born on 22 February 1929. If she'd glanced out of the bedroom window as she nursed him, John's mother Mary would have noticed sheep grazing in the fields. From the farmyard she would have heard the familiar sound of hooves ringing on the cobbles as heavy horses made their way to work.

Anyone looking out of the bedroom window at Sillywrea today would see the same sights and hear the same sounds. Inside the farmhouse, life's infinitely more comfortable. But outside, not much has changed in the intervening 70 odd years.

John's love of horses began early. He could only just walk when he went with his father one afternoon to a sale on a farm in the North Tyne Valley. George Dodd got into conversation with some farmers' wives. 'He was proud of his son and he wanted me to be on my best behaviour,' John says. 'But I saw the horses being led out of the stable to be sold and that was it. I was off! I can plainly remember running away and pushing myself between folks' legs to get to the front and watch what was happening.' Peering up at the giant animals through the rails of the sale ring, the boy felt no fear. It was only when his worried father came running after him that he realised the danger he might have been in.

At two, he was given a donkey, and at three a Shetland pony. 'Did I ride them? Oh yes. And I used to yoke the pony to an old sledge and get him to pull me round. The servant man who worked for us, Jack Dobson, nailed a couple of old trap shafts onto an axle with hay-heck wheels and fitted a box on the top. That was a great thing to ride on. I never took any harm, but it's a wonder I wasn't killed! I liked to copy the grown-ups. I can remember yoking three ponies in a line to pull some logs, just like the wood waggon drivers did.'

He was only eight when a pony he was galloping missed its footing and fell with John's leg under it. His ankle was broken, but what was worse, it was the beginning of the school holidays. He'd been looking forward to spending five weeks at home – but now he was unable to play with his ponies. He was able to indulge in another hobby, however. He bred ferrets and loved to go hobbling off for a day's rabbiting with a friend. 'He'd stand on one side of a stone wall and I'd guard the other, and the ferrets would chase the rabbits out of the wall. Many a time we'd be told off for pulling down the walls. But that was the way you were when you were young. You were so eager to get at the rabbits you'd scrabble away at the walls.'

Roaming the farm in search of rabbits, John got to know every field, and every wall that went round it. Sillywrea became his familiar kingdom.

Two Clydesdale mares from his childhood stand out in John's memory: Darling and Dinah. 'I can remember riding on old Darling's back while my father was walking behind, gathering up hay with a sweep. I'd be five or six. And I can remember sitting on my father's knee while he was working in the hay with an old Blackstone turner.' Dangerous? 'Well, not really Risks were taken, but a laddie learns best at that age. You never thought anything about it, although yes, I must confess it would be considered dangerous now.'

All the neighbouring farms had work horses, most of them Clydesdales, the breed which was the most popular in the north of England and Scotland. John's mind goes back to the first time he was allowed to plough. 'One of my relations was a farmer called Tom Heslop, of Farnley near Corbridge, about fifteen miles from here. One Saturday afternoon my mother and I were visiting "Uncle Tom" as we called him. I was about ten and I worshipped him. He was a great horseman and a wonderful ploughman.

'Well, we went out to the field where he was working. He set me between the stilts and let me hold the plough while he drove the horses and turned at the end of the row. It felt great, the strength of the horses and the easy way the plough glided through the soil. At that moment I was hooked. Even then, I could tell that if a plough is set properly, it'll more or less run by itself.'

By the time he was 11 John was doing grown-ups' work. At haytime, there was always a job for a lad leading in a horse and bogey laden with hay in from the field to the stack yard. Then he graduated to machines. He was allowed to drive a horsedrawn thistle cutter, his small frame perched on the machine's seat with the fearsome blade whirling beneath his feet. Horsedrawn machines were inherently dangerous, but farmers' sons like John were allowed to operate them – especially if they were persistent. 'I can remember it well,' John says. 'I whined and twisted on so much that my father eventually gave in.'

John went to the village school at the age of five. The teacher in the Infants class was a little chap called Tommy Hare. A marvellous schoolmaster, but somewhat given to exaggeration. 'He used to say when he was a little lad he never went to the dentist. Someone just came round with a hammer and chisel and knocked your teeth out. Well, you can imagine the effect that had on us children. We were horrified!'

On one occasion a boy called Jack Dobson from Staward missed some days because of the winter storms. When he got back Hare asked him what was wrong. Where had he been? When Jack blamed his absence on the snow, the diminutive Hare said: 'Fiddlesticks. When I went to school I waded through drifts right up to my neck.' Jack: 'I said nowt, but I thought it still wouldn't be very deep!'

John recalls another time when a big, raw-boned pupil at the school was being taken to task by the teacher. 'Hare was trying to cane George and the lad was just booting him around the blackboard.' But the teacher had the last laugh. He sent a note home to George's parents and later the boy told John ruefully: 'I was strang enough for Hare but I wasn't strang enough for me father.'

The teacher who replaced Hare was called Heslop. 'Army fellow,' John remembers. 'Still had his army cane and all. He sorted us out. There was no nonsense with Heslop.'

Teaching a boy whose thoughts were far away was frustrating for the schoolmaster. 'John Dodd,' he said once, 'you haven't heard a word I've been saying. You've just been staring out of the window.'

Young John wasn't daydreaming, however. He'd been watching the farmer harrowing the field next to the school. 'I couldn't tell the teacher what he'd been saying,' John smiles, 'but I could have told him how many times Fred Common had turned his horses. I could have told him what the horses' names were and where they had been bought. And I could have told him what crop they were putting in. You see, I was much more interested in that than school work.'

John left school at 14. He hadn't passed the exam to get into the grammar school. 'I didn't really like school,' he says. 'Arithmetic I didn't mind but I hated spelling. Mind, if I had to go back now I would maybe try and do better. It wasn't that I was a dunce. I was just like a wild bird in a cage. My mind was always on something else outside the school.'

In those days farmers' oldest sons were expected to follow in their fathers' footsteps and eventually take over the farm. The younger ones were sent to work for someone else. The hope was that one day they might get a small farm of their own too.

Being an only son John knew he was destined to work with his father George. But believing his son needed to learn some additional skills George Dodd paid for him to go to Telfords' joiners and undertakers firm in nearby Haydon Bridge. 'Grand family,' John says. 'Great joiners. With hindsight it did me a lot of good. Naturally, you can't learn everything about joinery in a twelvemonth, but it gave me a rough idea of how to handle the tools. And I learned how to work.'

Luckily, he didn't have to do any undertaking work – unlike another lad, two years older, who was also serving his time at Telfords. One day the boy had to accompany his boss to a house where someone had just died. As they lowered the corpse into the coffin it let out what sounded like a mournful sigh, but was in fact just trapped wind escaping from the lungs. 'The lad was out of the room, down the stairs and into the street before the undertaker could blink an eye,' John says. 'He was scared stiff!'

At 15, John was back home and working with horses. 'The first spring I harrowed all the corn and did some ploughing. And the following year I raised drills for the turnips for the first time. I was straight into the routine of working hard.' He recalls evenings spent in the stable, cleaning and oiling harness. Those days, it seems, everything was done to a much higher standard. 'I seemed to work all the time,' says John.

'Work was pretty much my hobby. In our spare time we had whist drives and concerts in the village hall, and there were dances too, although I was never a dancer. I suppose that, mostly, I liked being at home and liked being with the horses.'

Sillywrea before the Second World War was an all-grass farm with no arable crops. With only livestock to look after there was just one unmarried 'servant lad' (farm labourer) working alongside John and his father. He lived in the farmhouse and was paid 17 shillings and sixpence a week (about 87p) plus his keep (board and lodging). It was equal to about 30 shillings (£1.50) a week.

In common with all the farmers in the district, the Dodds hand-milked a few cows, reared calves and made butter. The cattle were Shorthorns, and like all dairy cattle at that time, they had – as their name implies – a splendid pair of horns. In some areas of the north the value of a cow (less than £20 in the 1930s) depended as much on the tilt of its horns and its colour as on its milking qualities. The favourite colour for Shorthorn cows was light roan. But having a black nose was considered to be a sign of poor stock. Such were the fashions in cattle breeding at the time.

When war began, everything in the countryside stepped up a gear. The 1930s had been a decade of depression on Britain's farms. Low prices had forced many farmers into bankruptcy and if a farm came up to let there were often no takers at all. All that changed in 1939. Farmers were told to plough as much land as possible as part of the Dig for Victory campaign. On the orders of the Northumberland War Agricultural Committee, 50 acres of grass (a quarter of the whole farm) went under the plough at Sillywrea.

'The war changed a lot of things,' John recalls. 'We seemed to work even harder. Nights when I came home from school, weekends, holidays. They wanted us to produce, and we responded.'

Land girls based in a hostel at Haydon Bridge helped on the farm. They threw themselves into the unfamiliar work, bringing with them a sense of fun. John and Maggie are still in regular touch with one, Paddy, now a widow in her seventies. 'The majority of them were very good,' he remembers. 'When you think that they were just shop girls and factory workers before the war and how they came onto the farms, threshing, spreading muck, milking cows, forking sheaves, you couldn't help but take your hat off to them. They were marvellous. And hoeing turnips, by Jove, a row of them hoeing turnips was quite a sight. Some of them made very fine hoers.'

John holds the view that some of the post-war antagonism directed towards farmers by city-dwellers has its roots in the 1939-45 conflict. Farmers' sons and some farm workers were exempt from military service because they were supposed to be doing their bit for Britain by producing food. 'Try telling that to someone who had lost two or three sons in the fighting, sons who had been conscripted and had no choice,' says John. 'No wonder there was resentment. It was only natural. It's only my opinion, but I think it did contribute towards the dislike some people have of farmers. It was the start of the widening gulf between town and country.'

As his teenage years advanced, John took on more and more of the horse work. He liked to ride the Clydesdales, as well as working them. Coming home from the ploughing at dinner time, there seemed to be no point in walking behind them, when he could jump up and get a ride. Other ploughmen used to ride side saddle, but not John. He always preferred to ride astride.

He was much more at home on a horse than his father was. 'For all my father liked horses, he was never the horseman or ploughman I was,' John says. 'He liked to breed Bluefaced Leicester sheep and Shorthorn cattle. He won prizes at a lot of shows before the war. But he wasn't as keen on horses as I was.'

The pattern of work was the same: up early and work till late. It's a habit that's continued to this day. 'It's a family farm, always was,' John says. 'But you just wonder how much longer these family farms can last. They say the wheel always turns but at the moment there isn't a big future for farms like this.

'Some people say they're the cheapest run farms of all because you work for nothing. At one time a son or daughter worked for pocket money and the farm was sure to come to them at the end. But that day has passed. Right from when I started to work on the farm I was always paid a wage. My father said I should be on a sound footing.'

Is a love of horses innate, or is it inherited? John is pretty sure he knows where his interest stems.

'Grandfather Dodd was a good hand with the horses and they reckon that's who I took after. It's been my life to work with horses.

It's bred in me, it's the way I'm made, simple as that. If I had my life over again I'd still work with horses.'

Grandfather Dodd was a man who, like John, was an individualist. He was a butcher's son, but he decided at an early age he'd rather work on the land than trim joints of meat. As a young man of 14 he turned his back on the family business and made for the woodlands where he earned a meagre living stripping bark off oak trees for use in the dyers' trade. 'A hard life,' John says. 'Piece work, so much a bag for the bark. I don't know how long he was in the woods. Probably until he grew strong. And then he went and worked on the farms. He was horseman at Shortmoor, near Wark, and horseman at Ellfoot near Haydon Bridge, and after that he got the managership at Wylam Drift colliery farm before renting a farm at Warden. My father never liked that farm, it was too enclosed for him. He wanted some space and he moved to Prior House. It was more out-bye. Then he married my mother and came to live at Sillywrea. That was in 1928. She'd been running the family farm for two years with her widowed mother, with hired labour, of course. All the same, it was a hard job for a couple of women in the 1920s.'

John's father retired in 1964 but struggled on, crippled by arthritis, until he died a week before his 84th birthday in 1983. 'To begin with he helped a bit after he retired,' John recalls. 'He'd get a bale of hay on a fork over his shoulder and with his stick in his other hand go and feed a beast, but it was a struggle for him.'

Left alone on the farm, it might have been an opportunity for John to replace horse-power on four legs with horsepower provided by four wheels, but he had no desire to get rid of his Clydesdales. 'I never really gave it a thought,' he says. 'I don't think they're cheaper to run, but in terms of capital invested they're cheaper. You only have to bring a new tractor home from the dealers and it's starting to lose money. Whereas horses cost a lot less. But it's not just a financial thing. It's both work and pleasure, working with horses. It's my favourite job on the farm.'

Interest in heavy horses seems to fluctuate. When there's an oil crisis, as there was in the 1970s, people talk enthusiastically about getting rid of their tractors and going back to horses. But it doesn't seem to last long. 'There's no doubt about it,' John says, 'if young chaps coming in to farming were working with horses it would be a much cheaper way of starting. But the fact is they don't have the experience. Or the interest. They don't seem to realise how much pleasure it is, or how much work a pair of horses can get through.'

By 1975, with no son to help, John was beginning to rely more and more on Frances, who'd left school at 16, to help him. But he didn't stint himself when it came to graft. 'When it was just myself and Frances working the farm, I'd be up at half past four in the morning in winter and have all the byres mucked out before breakfast. Two hours it took. Black dark. And after breakfast I'd be off ploughing until it got dark again at night. I thought nothing of it. Getting up early's nothing, you know. It's just the thought of it that puts you off.'

Frances and her mother are accepting of John's all-embracing passion for work. But that doesn't stop them having a smile or two at his expense. One summer's day they stood at the kitchen window watching him turn a field of hay with one of his horses. It had started to drizzle. Most farmers would have packed up and gone home. But not John.

'Mastermind,' said Frances.

'Mastermind?' her mother queried.

'I've started, so I'll finish,' said Frances

44

drily. 'That's Dad's attitude!'

Having his son-in-law David helping him has been a boost for John. 'He's taken to the horses, and he's a great hand with them,' he says. 'He does most of the heavy work now.'

In his mid-60s John suffered a heart attack. Like all such life-threatening events, it made him pause and take stock for a while. But work is the very essence of his being, and he found it hard to take things easy. 'I can still do most of the jobs I used to do. Lifting things isn't a problem. The only things that bother me are getting vexed and hurrying on a cold day. That sets the angina going whiles.'

If anything does vex John, it's the change in Government policy towards farming in the last 60 years. It was ominous for farmers, he says, when the Ministry of Agriculture was swallowed up by the Department of Environment, Food and Rural Affairs in June 2001. Farming's role was undoubtedly downgraded.

'After the war all the cry was: farmers must produce more. That's what we've done for 60 years. It's what the politicians wanted.

'In truth, everyone would like to keep fewer stock, not more. It would make life easier and be better for the land. But we've been running to stand still for years.

'People write letters to the papers saying what's happened recently is the farmers' own fault and it's the farmers' greed. But farmers have had to keep more stock just to exist.'

Subsidies have been a part of farming for half a century, but there are those who believe the industry would have been better off without them. John likes to quote the well-known pre-war farming writer, A.G. Street whose book *Farmer's Glory*, published in 1932, charted the changes he had witnessed in a quarter of a century of farming. 'Street was the only man who ever wrote against subsidies. He said we'd live to rue the day we ever accepted them. And mind, it's just about come true. If the price of our produce had been allowed to rise at the same rate as inflation there wouldn't have been a need for subsidies.'

Although his business is influenced by decisions made far away in Whitehall and Brussels, John is happiest when concentrating on working his land. How long does he think he will go on for? He answers: 'I don't do as much as I used to on the farm. The truth is, I can't. But I've had a happy life. I'll do what I can – as long as I can. So long as my health keeps good.'

John sees himself as custodian of Silly-

46

wrea. 'Nothing is more honest than land,' he says. 'I believe a good farmer should leave a farm in better heart than it was when he took it over.'

In the Bible (Ecclesiastes 1:2) it is written: 'One generation passeth away and another generation cometh, but the earth abideth for ever.' John agrees: 'I always say the land is more important than the people. People are just here for a time but the land is here for ever. No one has the right to misuse the land. And this is what I say about the horses. If I thought the land was taking harm through sticking with the horses, I would change straightaway. But the only way the land could take any harm was by not getting the jobs done in season. As long as we can get the jobs done in season with the horses, well, there's no way the land can suffer.'

Maggie Dodd

It's sometimes hard to comprehend the scale on which life in rural Northumberland has altered over the past century. There have been so many changes in employment patterns, so many improvements in living conditions. Whereas a large part of the population was involved in farming 100 years ago, today many of the places those families occupied are no longer farms but 'barn conversions', where newcomers to the countryside enjoy a comfortable rural lifestyle with none of the deprivations of the 19th century.

When Maggie Dodd looks back over her four score years she says that, by and large, she's been happy. But there was hardship in her early years, and there has been sadness and loss too. She was born Margaret Elizabeth Hall on 11 March 1921, the youngest of a family of eight and the only one who is now still alive. The family lived in a two-bedroom house at Langley sawmill, about a mile from where she now lives.

Her father, Jimmy, drove wood waggons pulled by teams of Clydesdale horses. His job was dragging logs out of forests. 'There were always seven or eight horses at our place,' she remembers. 'My father was a great hand with the horses. They were all constantly handled and talked to, almost like members of the family. Just like John's horses.'

John says: 'Jimmy Hall was a legendary wood-waggon man. He didn't just pull out thinnings, it was big stuff: oak, ash and beech trees. It was a hard life for a horse in the woods, yet he had horses that lived 16 or 17 years. He was a generous feeder and looked after them well.'

With such a big family, life wasn't easy but by scrimping and saving Mrs Hall managed to make ends meet. Maggie didn't always see eye to eye with her mother. How many daughters do? But she says proudly: 'Mother brought a family up and never owed a penny, even though the biggest pay my father brought home was only £2 a week. That took some doing in those days.'

A lot of the Halls' social life revolved round going to chapel and calling in on the numerous members of the family spread round the district. Some of Maggie's more ancient relatives were born back in the late 1800s and it seemed to her as a child that they'd grown up in a different age. She recalls visiting an elderly great-aunt on a remote hill farm above Allendale in the 1920s. Wearing a man's cap, as many daleswomen still did at that time, the old lady held court in her warm, dimly-lit kitchen. 'As soon as you walked in she would say to one of the men: "Give the lassie a batty" and he would reach up above the fireplace for the biscuit tin. She always called biscuits "batties". It's an old-fashioned word you rarely hear now.

'People were always popping in. They'd call for a cup of tea and end up staying for supper. Your tins were always full of fruit cake and gingerbread. And everyone walked miles in those days. My auntie worked 57 years in private service for the same family. They had a big house on the far side of Hexham. There was a railway line though here at that time – it's closed now, of course. On her half day she would come up on the train to see her family and when she'd finished she'd walk back to where she worked – in all weathers. It was a good eight miles. But she couldn't afford the train fare both ways, so she just had to take to the road. It's so different today. If you see someone walking up the road you think there's something wrong!'

Few people had their own cars. For food, families in outlying places relied on what they could grow, what they could harvest from the countryside (wild raspberries, mushrooms, crab apples) and supplies from the travelling vans. Fortunately, in the days before fridges became commonplace, these called frequently: 'We had Allendale Co-op van with groceries on a Monday; Birketts the bakers came on a Tuesday; Chesters, the family bakers, called on Wednesdays and Saturdays; Elliotts – they were another firm of bakers – came on Thursdays, and the butcher's van called on Fridays. Large loaves were threepence halfpenny (about one penny today). Imagine that. You pay 79 pence for the same loaf today.

'My happiest childhood memory is of Easter. On Good Friday Birketts used to deliver hot cross buns at seven in the morning, and mind, they were hot! Just been baked and lovely with plenty of butter. And then a woman in the village used to come round and give all the kiddies an orange and a paice egg.'

These were eggs that had been hardboiled in onion skins or vegetable dye. Children would bowl them against each other until the shells cracked, a tradition which continues to this day in some places in the north.

Watching how her mother did it, Maggie learned to cook, darn and sew. She was expected to. Meanwhile, she was attending the village school half a mile away, where 50 pupils aged from five to 14 were packed into two small classrooms. Maggie remembers it all in vivid detail: 'All the lads wore clogs. You could hear them coming up the road a mile away, clip clopping. And if they'd lost an iron off the bottom of the clog it was a different ring. The steps sounded uneven.'

Maggie enjoyed her years at the village school and passed the exam to go to the local grammar school, where one of her brothers was already a pupil. But to her dismay, her family couldn't afford to buy a uniform for her. These were harsh times and there was no other choice: she had to go out and earn her living. So at the age of 14, Maggie left home and started work as a servant girl on a local farm, West Land Ends. 'All the farm houses had a servant girl and a servant lad living in,' she says. 'People needed help. There was such a lot to do.'

In an era long before the introduction of labour-saving machines, it was hard graft from the moment the day began: 'You had to take out the ashes, sweep the hearth, light the fire and make the porridge,' remembers Maggie. 'Then you had to rub the cast-iron kitchen range with black lead and polish the fender. The range at that first farm, why, it was the biggest I'd ever seen. It seemed to take an age to clean it. It looked lovely when you'd finished but you blessed (cursed) it while you were doing it. And in the scullery, they had a massive sink, as big as a table, for washing up in. In the majority of places water was to carry in. No bathrooms or turning taps in those days. Just water from a well or a trough.'

In her spare time, Maggie met up with other people of her age. There seemed to be no shortage of things to do: 'You made your own enjoyment. The young ones seemed far happier then than they do today. After chapel on Sunday nights we thought nothing of going out on the country roads, just sauntering along and talking. Then there were the Saturday night "hops" and whist drives at the village hall. Everyone came from far and wide on their pushbikes.'

In 1936, Maggie got a job as servant girl at Sillywrea. She was just 15. 'We knew the Dodds, they were neighbours,' she recalls. 'I was happy about going there.' The indoor routine continued: washing on Monday, baking on Tuesday. Cooking, cleaning, brushing, polishing. Ironing was done on the kitchen table on a white cloth, with a blanket underneath to stop the table from being scorched. The flat irons were heated by the fire.

Outside the farmhouse, there were other duties, like milking the cows. 'No one ever taught you. It just came naturally to you. Sitting on a three-legged stool with the bucket between your knees, you were always expecting the cows to lash out with their feet. That was why you used to talk to them – so they knew you and didn't kick.' She laughs. 'I don't think cows nowadays would let you do that.'

Making butter was a notoriously unpredictable business. Maggie's mother would stand the milk in a bowl and ladle the cream off with a saucer. Then it was churned to make it into butter. 'Sometimes it came easy, other times it didn't,' says Maggie. 'In hot weather the cream often wouldn't turn and all your efforts had been wasted.'

Pig killing day was a special event. It was always at 'the backend' (the end of the year) in time for the cooler weather of winter, when the meat would last longer without going off. 'We used to buy blocks of salt a foot wide and a foot high, and scrape the salt off with knives and crush it with a rolling pin. It was a hard job. That was a day's work in itself – before the pig killing.' The salt was to rub into sides of bacon which were then hung on hooks in the kitchen to be preserved. The old saying 'Everything but the squeak' was certainly true: nothing was wasted at a pig killing. Blood was used to make black pudding, and all the leftovers went into bowls of brawn.

Sausages were made by scraping and scalding the pigs' intestines and stuffing them with meat from the mincer. 'It was a great occasion, pig killing. Most farms round here did two at once and then they had "home-killed" to give away to all their family and friends. One lady in the village, Miss Dinning – Auntie Minnie we called her – was very kind. She used to send the servant lad or girl round with a butter-basket and leave sausage, potted meat or spare ribs at every house in the village. She was a lovely person. We often used to wonder if she'd kept enough for herself!'

John and Maggie knew each other at school so when she came to work for his parents it was like a reunion with a friend. Over the years the friendship blossomed and, eventually, they decided to get married. The wedding day was 12 June 1954. At that moment, Maggie went from employee to wife. She and John settled in at Harlowfield, a farmhouse belonging to the family on the edge of Sillywrea's land. They've been there ever since. 'John's always said I got a bonus when I left,' she laughs merrily. 'Him!'

Humour has been a thread which has run through their lives. Maggie loves to hear John's tales about old farming characters from the surrounding area. She laughs happily at the memories they bring back. On one wall of the kitchen hangs a plaque: 'Don't question my wife's judgement – Look who she married.' It shows John doesn't take himself too seriously.

His parents gave Maggie a dozen hens as a wedding present and she's kept poultry ever since. In the early days of her marriage Maggie used to pickle eggs for the winter – the time when the hens weren't laying. 'The old hens drop off, but then I get some pullets and they start to lay,' she says. 'I still like my hens. I look forward to letting them out every day and seeing what they've laid.'

Initially Maggie helped a lot on the farm, but she's always left horse work to others. 'Horses have played a big part in my life but they always seemed to have too many feet and legs for me. I dreaded walking down the road with them. John once got me to take a pair of horses down from the field to the farmyard. I was frantic – those great big feet stepping beside me. He said he'd come and meet me but he didn't. I think he was trying to break me in but I haven't had a lot to do with them since then.'

At haymaking time, Maggie would always appear in the field at quarter to four with a picnic for John and the workers, who were too busy to come back to the farm. A basket full of sandwiches and cakes, and tea in a pot, all laid out on a cloth in the hay. Her family remember with affection the time when they asked Maggie to go beyond her usual role – and join in at the end of the day's haymaking. 'They wanted me to go with a horse and take the last load of bales from the field. I was fair petrified. I had the whole field to turn round in. But blow me, I knocked over the only heap of bales that was left! They've never let me live it down. John loves to tell people about the day I knocked the bales down.'

But while there was joy at Sillywrea, there was sorrow too. In April 1969, John and Maggie lost their only son Edwin through leukaemia. Maggie remembers the day it began. 'He took ill one Saturday in August. He only lived eight months after that, but he never once complained. He was just 14 when he died.

'He was a quiet lad, very reserved really He'd just started at the high school and he was coming out of his shell a bit. But he was reserved and all for staying at home. He didn't like to go away anywhere.'

John says: 'He never ailed a thing in his life

before then. There was no warning of what he was going to get. He worked with the horses; he was leading bales and turning hay at 12. By, he could handle horses just like a man. He was a natural horseman.

'It was Allendale Show day when he took sick, and unfortunately he never recovered. It was a big blow for all of us. Part of our life was snatched away.'

A simple marble headstone in the graveyard at Haydon Bridge cemetery commemorates Edwin's short life. The inscription reads: 'Safe in the arms of Jesus.'

Maggie: 'It's hard. But in time you learn to accept it, you do. Frances was just 11 at the time. It went hard with her. Edwin could do no wrong, he was the apple of her eye. She just took over and did what Edwin would have done. Frances has loved horses all her life. She can do anything with them.'

John: 'Frances stepped in. She was a great help. She got to know how to handle horses and she sowed turnips, cut grass and led hay with the bogeys. You had to admire her. She did practically everything.'

Edwin's death left an aching hole in their lives. John threw himself into work. Maggie devoted herself to the traditional home-making activities of a farmer's wife. The year's calendar continued, as it does in farming.

There was a constant battle to try and make the farmhouse kitchen a warmer place. Evidence of this lies on the floor, which is strewn with Maggie's colourful 'stobby' mats. Old clothes were cut up into strips and a thick hooked needle was used to pull them through holes in a canvas fixed to a frame. When canvas was too expensive, old hessian wheat sacks were used.

'My mother and my aunt used to sit all winter making mats,' Maggie recalls. 'They aimed to make two big hearth rugs each, and the newest one would be spread closest to the fire where everyone could admire it.'

The mats were all kinds of designs. Hooky mats were made along the same lines, except that they used lengths of wool unravelled from old jumpers. Maggie points to one on the floor leading to her back kitchen. 'That's a hooky mat made by my mother in 1934,' she says. 'And it's still wearing well.'

Proud though she may be of her mother's mat-making prowess, Maggie still recalls a childhood moment associated with making stobby mats that hurt her at the time. 'I was a child no bigger than my grandson Richard when I overheard my mother talking to my auntie about the mats they were making. I'd just come in the back door and I was standing, as children do, in the passage listening to the grown-ups' conversation. Mother said to my auntie: "What are we going to do with that square that Maggie did?" It obviously wasn't up to their high standards. So my auntie said: "Wait until she goes to bed and we'll pull it out." I've never forgotten that. I always vowed I'd never make a stobby mat with them. But I made plenty when I got my own home.'

Maggie still has an unfinished stobby mat on her frame, but she's somewhat daunted by the thought of completing it. 'I'm not sure if I'll go back to making mats at my age,' Maggie says. 'It's so time-consuming, and it's quite hard work. But in the old days, when money was scarce, you had to make things which didn't cost anything. That's how I learned how to make mats. You just grew up with these traditions.'

Maggie still keeps up some of her traditional cooking habits. Autumn is a time for pickling onions. 'Mother always did a lot of pickled onions. Of course in those days we grew them in the garden: shallots. I usually start in September and do some for the harvest festival. For a charity they're a good money-spinner. I always like to keep a jar or two in the house. Mind, I'm not sure who else pickles onions these days. I've never heard tell of anyone else round here but me!'

If peeling onions upsets you, Maggie has a good tip to stop your eyes watering: 'Mother always said you should sit as close to the fire as possible when you're peeling onions. You know, I find it works. I never seem to shed a tear. Someone also once told me you should hold a crust of bread in your mouth when you're peeling onions, but that didn't work for me. I had the bread eaten long before I had the onion peeled!'

One dish Maggie has always refused to make is 'spotted dick', suet pudding with raisins in it. 'Mother used to make them as big as footballs and put them down in front of us. The child that ate the most pudding got the most meat, but by the time you'd eaten your portion of pudding you were too full. Maybe that was the idea. But I vowed that when I got a house of my own the one thing I'd never cook would be spotted dick.'

Maggie accepts that John, like most farmers, works long hours, and she doesn't mind. Nor does she mind the part horses have played in his life. 'It's lovely really, because quite frankly the horses all know him. He talks to them as though they were his best friends, well, maybe they are! In a way I think it helped him after he had his heart attack. He would go to a horse and talk to it and take his mind off his own problems.'

Things that townspeople take for granted came slowly to Langley. It wasn't until 1958 that Maggie switched on her first electric light. Before power supplies arrived in the district her house was lit by lamps and candles.

Maggie doesn't miss the hardships she experienced in her early years, but she does miss some of the features of country life that have vanished for good. A particular regret is the disappearance of the travelling vans. One by one they all stopped making their rounds, until the only survivor was the hardware man who came once a fortnight with a van stuffed with everything from cloths to pins. Then, three years ago, he called it a day.

'We've many good friends, and people still call in and say hello,' she says. 'But it isn't like it used to be when I was young. There seemed to be so many people about in the countryside in those days.'

Frances Wise

The highest point of the farm is only about 700 feet above sea level, but because of the way the land lies you can see for miles in all directions. From here, on a clear morning at the beginning of April 2001, Frances could glimpse black palls of smoke rising from fires in five different points in a circle round Sillywrea. They were funeral pyres where cattle slaughtered because of Foot and Mouth Disease were being burned. For anyone who loves animals, as Frances does, it was a deeply upsetting sight.

Throughout the spring of 2001 Foot and Mouth crept closer and closer to Sillywrea. Like most farmers in counties like Northumberland, which are primarily stock-rearing regions, John and his family felt they were under siege. A thick piece of carpet soaked in disinfectant lay across the entrance to the farm. Visitors were told not to call. Footpaths across the farm were closed.

Information about the spread of the disease wasn't easy to obtain. The picture was confusing. There were 'confirmed cases', farms whose animals had been affected by the disease. There were 'contiguous culls' on farms which shared boundaries with infected farms. And there were 'dangerous contacts' – farms within a three-kilometre radius of infected farms, whose sheep, cattle and pigs were killed as a precaution, even though they were un-touched by the disease.

From watching the local news on television and radio, Frances was able to keep track of the progress of Foot and Mouth. She picked up a lot more from phone calls to farming friends. The feelings people expressed were mostly of anger and disbelief. Anger at the way the epidemic had been handled; disbelief over the huge number of healthy animals that had been wiped out.

The scars left by the Foot and Mouth outbreaks of 2001 are deep. One day Frances drove past a nearby farm, where the disease had been confirmed that morning. In one of the fields, sheep were still grazing. 'I noticed a ewe that had not long given birth. Her two lambs stood on wobbly legs, beginning to hunt for their first suck of milk. Their mother was licking them, no doubt "talking" to them in her own language so that they would learn to recognise her "voice". I cried with the knowledge of their future.

'Coming home that evening, I looked into that same field. It was empty. The sheep and lambs had been slaughtered. The sheep troughs were lined up in rows but there were no animals to use them. It was very poignant. That's what haunted me for the next days and weeks. Those empty troughs.'

It affected Frances to such an extent that, not for the first time in her life, she felt moved to express her feelings in poetry:

The field stands empty
Surrounded by signs of emerging spring:
Spindly shrub and sturdy tree
Fringe their limbs with shades of green
As, nourished by roots sunk deep
They waken from winter's sleep.
The spreading cloak of foliage will screen
Birds which, with lengthening days,
Have flitted, flirted, courted
And now with nests complete
Sing their songs of praise
And wait for this year's brood.
The field stands empty
No mouths 'cept those of rabbit or deer
To nibble the grass
Which grows greener, sweeter.

Sheep troughs wait for ghosts of ewes
Which only yesterday
Jostled greedily at shepherd's feet,
Heavy bellies and swelling udders
Indicating imminent birth.
Lambs, symbols of spring,
The promise of continuing life
From Mother Earth.
But their lives were cut short
Ended by slaughtermen's guns.
Silent as the emerging green
Foot and Mouth Disease
Unwanted and unseen
Came to Castle Farm.
Now there's no flock, no herd
All are gone
And the field stands empty

The diseased farm was less than two miles from Sillywrea. David, Frances and her parents feared the worst. By rights, the animals in a ring of farms surrounding the outbreak would have to be killed: a total of 4000 sheep and several hundred cattle. But the weeks went by and no order to slaughter was issued. Had an administrative error allowed their animals to escape? There was a feeling of relief, but it was difficult, for Frances who felt sympathy for farming families in a worse plight.

Generations of farming folk
Lifetimes' work gone up in smoke
Or buried deep within a pit
Grown men cry at the sight of it.
Such desolation cannot last
We've lost the future, lost the past
Lost into the dark abyss
What acts of folly led to this?
Disease or cull, it ends the same
Where's the reason, where's the blame?
Oh, where will it end? When will it end?
We have the questions, have you the
    answers, my friend?
Farmers, walkers, tourist trade
All want firm guidance to be made
But 'experts' talk, act with indecision
While worry, frustration create deep
    division.
Families struggle alone and bereft
To pick up the pieces of life that are left;
A life that's changed at such terrible cost
And communities mourn a spring that's
    been lost.

'I've always wanted to write more,' Frances says. 'I've written poems in the past, but normally it's hard to find the time. Somehow, the Foot and Mouth epidemic made me want to put it down in words once again.'

Her poetry was an expression of the emotions she was feeling as the crisis unfolded. 'I found it easier to cope with it all when we were in the thick of lambing, because we were so busy and we knew the stock were healthy. We couldn't believe it would happen to us. But as lambing eased off there was more time to think – and more time to worry.'

Because of the farm's proximity to a confirmed outbreak, a 'Form D' notice was issued, forbidding movements of all animals to and from Sillywrea. 'That's when it started to really hit me,' says Frances.

I don't feel like smiling today
Don't feel cheery and bright,
So I won't join in your laughter
Your fun, your games
Somehow, it wouldn't feel right.

I do feel like crying today,
Past sadness, future fears.
Don't you see the suffering,
The struggle, the pain?
Do you understand my fears?

I'm tired of just keeping going
Of being positive and strong
Of wondering and worrying
What if or why?
But you, the world, have moved on.

In late August 2001 came the development
Frances and her family had been dreading.
After three months of being clear of foot and
mouth, Northumberland was again hit by a
series of outbreaks, all of them clustered
round the town of Allendale which is not far
from Sillywrea. As the book went to print,
the disease was less than a mile away.

Frances came into the world in the maternity
wing of Haltwhistle War Memorial Hospital
on 17 September 1957. Her brother Edwin
was already two-and-a-half. She remembers
her childhood as being happy – and one in
which, inevitably, horses played their part.
Like her father before her, she had a Shetland pony. She learned to ride at a young age.
   The village school at Langley, where her
parents had met, closed shortly before
Frances was due to start school, so at the age
of four she began her education at the Shafto
Trust School in Haydon Bridge, four miles
away. At the age of ten she took the 11-plus

and gained a place at Hexham Grammar School.

While Frances enjoyed non-agricultural pursuits like playing the piano, Edwin threw himself into life on the farm. He and Frances enjoyed a typically robust relationship. 'We were a normal brother and sister. We fought a lot, but at the same time we stuck up for each other at school. Blood's thicker than water, isn't it?'

It was only when Edwin died that Frances started to play a larger role on the farm. Her father taught her how to handle the horses and she became adept at driving the huge animals. She left school at 16 after taking her 'O' levels and started to work full time with her father. In 1975, so as to master the business side of farming, she enrolled on a farm secretary's course at the Northumberland College of Agriculture. It was a year which culminated in her one and only trip abroad – a week with a group of students visiting farms in France in the summer of 1976. 'I came back and found my father had finished the hay on his own,' she recalls. 'It was the best haytime in living memory.'

Working long hours with heavy horses, you become attached to them. But you have to reconcile yourself to the inevitability of their demise. Frances was particularly fond of Prince, a part-Shire who was as loyal as the day is long. But on a warm July day in 1982 Prince, aged 13, collapsed and died of a brain haemorrhage while pulling a hay turner. The shock of losing one of her favourite horses prompted one of Frances' early poems.

Today Prince has left us
For that life beyond our ken
Where reins of gold will guide him
And angels instead of men.

Oh but we will miss him
No longer about the place
Gentle giant of a horse
We'll ne'er forget his face.
Aye but he was a character
A torment, and a tease
But a loved friend and workmate
So Lord, take care of him please.

Despite her close bond with the farm and its horses, Frances decided she should maintain as much contact with the outside world as possible. One day a week, she worked as a clerk for Hexham Auction Mart Company. 'I loved it,' she says, 'especially the big sheep sales at Bellingham when all the North Tyne farmers and shepherds used to come to the mart. It was great meeting all the buyers and sellers. It was sociable. There were so many great characters.'

Frances continued to combine her work on the farm with her day at the mart. But in the meantime there was a new presence in her life. He was David Wise, a tall young man she'd first spotted in a Young Farmers Club drama production, and who she got to know through the church they both attended. David worked on a farm a few miles away and they shared interests in farming and the countryside. Their friendship grew, and they went out together for a number of years before wedding bells rang out on 2 April 1988. David began working at Sillywrea and he and Frances began their married life together in the large farmhouse built in 1870 by John's great-grandfather. Also still living there was Mary Dickinson, John's mother, who'd been widowed five years previously.

On 14 July 1989 there was joy for the family when Frances gave birth to Richard. She was now very much at the start of another new phase of her life. As well as continuing to help with the farm animals and keeping an eye on her grandmother, she was also coping with being a mother.

Twelve years on, Richard is a rapidly-growing youngster who loves life on the farm. But Frances' grandmother is now a rather confused 98-year-old who has to be visited regularly by carers. She spends occasional weeks in a local residential home to give her family some respite. But the rest of the time it's up to Frances to look after her.

The responsibility has curbed another of Frances' creative skills, for the time being at least. As well as writing and playing the piano, she's spent long hours producing dozens of beautifully iced cakes for festive occasions of all kinds: birthdays, weddings, Christmas. It all goes back to a childhood visit to a chrysanthemum show in a school in the nearby town of Hexham: 'I can remember going into a classroom where the iced cakes were and thinking they were absolutely wonderful. The detail was fantastic. So when I got a bit older I started fiddling on with icing. Then I went to night classes a few times and after that it was just practice, and learning by your mistakes. I don't think I'm very good, but I seem to do well enough for most people! It's very satisfying when you can see they're pleased with them.'

Sometimes people give her designs to copy, but she prefers to have a free rein and produce something from her own imagination. And of course, the consistency of the icing has to be right. Frances recalls being at a wedding once where the bride and groom were out of the room for what seemed to be an age while they cut the cake. (Not one of hers, she hastens to add.) Eventually they reappeared with lumps of icing and a pile of crumbs: the icing was so hard that the cake had eventually disintegrated. 'So we all received a serviette with a few crumbs and a lump of icing, and the whole room fell silent as people tried to consume the icing. It was as though we'd all bought a bag of gobstoppers!'

Frances always ices her cakes in the evening. But it can be hazardous. On one warm autumn night she flung open the kitchen window before going into the sitting room to watch television, leaving three freshly-iced cakes on the kitchen table. 'At about 10 o'clock at night I shouted to David: "Quick! Turn the outside lights on!" He soon realised why. The whole kitchen was full of moths fluttering around my newly-iced cakes. So we turned off the kitchen lights and the moths all flew out of the window. But it was a close thing.'

When she got married, Frances used all her

artistic flair to make a wonderful job of the icing on her own three-tier cake, decorating it with green ribbons to match the bridesmaids' dresses. And when the time came for her parents' friends Martin and Winnie Jackson to celebrate their 50th wedding anniversary, Frances again exercised her skills, designing a cream-coloured cake with gold ribbons and 50 golden roses.

'Over the years I've decorated lots of cakes,' she says. 'But unless it's a really special occasion, I haven't got the time to do them now. I still bake a lot. The tins are always full of cakes and scones. But icing cakes for other people is something I'll have to come back to some time in the future.'

Frances hasn't worked with the five horses which do the work at Sillywrea now. That job is left to the men. But her interest in the sheep continues unabated, and she's the one who's trained the sheepdogs to gather and sort.

The older one is Fly, a tricoloured six-year-old bitch bred by Peter Telfer, of Waite Farm, Haydon Bridge. 'I wouldn't claim to be a sheepdog trainer but I can get my dogs to work for me on our farm,' she says. 'Sheepdogs have a herding instinct, so I'll just wait and see what a dog will do and when it does it right, confirm that with a command. I don't use a whistle, I just shout. Gradually you get them to respond. Fly's a good worker, willing to please. I like working with her.'

Jan is a three-year-old bred by John Cleasby at Barton Church Farm, Tirril, near Penrith in Cumbria. This is the farm where John's newly-bought colt foals spent their first 18 months. 'He was looking for a home for this young bitch and we liked the look of her,' Frances recalls. 'She's fitted in really well because she's got a lovely nature. She's keen to work but she doesn't particularly like being given orders. She'd rather operate under her own steam. But a lot of sheepdogs are like that. You have to show them who's in charge.'

David Wise

'Most people have gone from the horses to the tractor,' John Dodd says, looking back over the last 50 years. 'But David's done it the other way round. He's gone from the tractor to the horses. And, by Jove, he's taken to them like a duck to water.'

To work side by side with a man steeped in the lore of heavy horses is a test as well as a pleasure. John's knowledge of horses is vast and David Wise has enjoyed learning from him. But John also has exacting standards when it comes to horse work, and in the 13 years he's been at Sillywrea David has had to strive hard to match those standards.

His father-in-law is in no doubt that David has succeeded. He says proudly: 'He's a grand chap. I'm delighted with him. Young horses need special handling and he's shown he can do that. He's capable of taking over the business or the work or anything.'

He may have taken to the land but David doesn't have soil running through his veins. He was born in Corbridge in Northumberland on 15 March 1954. His father was a doctor and many members of his family have been involved with medicine.

David's father moved around the northeast, eventually settling in the Washington area of Co. Durham, where David went to school. But he'd always been more interested in farming than anything else (he reckons one of his great-grandfathers, who kept goats, may have had something to do with it) and when he was young he used to go and stay with some relations, Anne and Brian Walker at Newbiggin Hill Farm in Hexhamshire. This is a picturesque area of south Northumberland which is sprinkled with small mixed farms. David loved looking after livestock so much that he spent every summer holiday there.

A year's day release at Houghall, the Co. Durham agricultural college, was followed by a two-year full-time course at the same college. Then, armed with technical know-how to back up the practical knowledge he'd picked up while staying on his relations' farm, David embarked on a life as a farm worker.

An affection for Hexhamshire drew him back to that district. He got a job on the Common family's farm, Low Ardley, and stayed there for three years before returning to Peterlee in County Durham for a while. It wasn't long before he was back at Low Ardley, however, and in his second spell at the farm he stayed 14 years.

Eventually chance led him to meet his future wife.

'I came to visit some relatives in Langley and they used to go to the chapel. That's where I first saw Frances.'

Not long afterwards the chapel needed reroofing. Worshippers had to find alternative accommodation for six weeks. As it happens, Frances is the chapel organist and there's a piano at Sillywrea, so it was decided to hold services in the farm sitting room for the time being. 'Naturally I was happy to go along to the farm,' smiles David. 'It was a chance to see Frances in her natural environment.'

At about the same time it began to dawn on John and Maggie that they were seeing a great deal of the fair-haired, blue-eyed farm worker from Hexhamshire.

At haytime, John's always had help from a few people who 'work loose' (casual) in the local area. 'Chaps that finish their work at five o'clock and drop in to lend a hand after they've had their tea.'

One year John was talking to David's uncle, who lives nearby. 'I said to him: "I think men are going to be hard to get a hold of for haytime this year." He says to me: "Why, David would like to come and help. Where he works they always finish their hay early. He'd like to see how you go on with the horses."

'So he came and helped.

'Well, as I said in my speech on their wedding day, I'm pretty slow on the uptake when it comes to courting and that type of thing. But I didn't take too long to realise that it wasn't just the horses David was coming to see, it was Frances as well!'

It was during one of those haytimes that David first took the reins of one of John's Clydesdales in his hands and walked behind the huge animal as it pulled a bogey along the farm lane to the hayfield for another load of bales. 'It just felt right,' he says. 'That first time I seemed to get along fine with the horses, and I just carried on from there. Frances and I courted for a number of years before we married, and all that time I used to come and help out whenever I could. For six months before the wedding I went self-employed and worked half the time for my old employers and half the time at Sillywrea.'

They married on 4 June 1988. 'Four-six-eight,' David laughs. 'Easy to remember!'

As he became absorbed into a life dominated by horses rather than the internal combustion engine, David felt more and more settled. He wasn't worried about the slower pace. In fact he began to relish it. He says: 'It's just all round enjoyment for me. I enjoy the steadier pace and the fact that there's less noise – no tractors rattling away. I spent half my working life with tractors and I have nothing against them, but I would be reluctant now to go back to them. I'm happy with horses and I feel I'm gaining enough experience with them to carry on should something happen to John.'

For someone from a non-horsey background, how did David learn? 'Practical experience and tuition from John. Having said that, he is very good at letting you get on by yourself, unless he can see that you're going to make a drastic mistake. He's always thinking of the safety of both yourself and the horses, so if you're going to get into a real mess he'll tell you so. But other than that, you pick it up as you go along.

'There's a tremendous amount to learn. I hadn't realised how much until I became involved. The horses themselves, the harness, the implements. How to yoke a horse up correctly so as it's not catching its heels and not rubbing against the shafts; not having the chains too short or too long because they can rub against the horse's legs and take the hair and then the skin off; what to look for if a horse goes lame; the horses' different characters.

'Horse-breaking I've learned primarily from watching John and then trying it myself. It sounds drastic but it isn't really. It's primarily getting the horse used to what you want it to do. First of all it's being handled, then getting used to wearing harness, then on to chains and shafts. Everything will feel different to the horse. You've got to know how to do it in a safe way both for yourself and the horse.

'You often hear the expression "gentle giants" used to describe Clydesdales, but I think it's a bit over-used. They can be gentle, but if you've got a fiery horse, you've got to be careful. Yes, some are fair old giants, but handled correctly and with care, you're all right. But they're not as quiet as some people think. It takes a lot of practice and experience to handle them well.'

David is aware that he and John are different. Sillywrea Farm is a one-off and they are virtually the last working horsemen.

He says modestly: 'We don't think of ourselves as unique, but there are very few farms now that genuinely still use horses day in day out. There are a lot of people who keep what we call hobby horses, which they use for showing and ploughing matches, but there's hardly any which are actually worked on a viable farm.

'I must admit, I feel proud of it. I don't feel we're set apart from the rest of the farming community, because the end product of what we do is just the same – we're still producing lamb for market, beef for market, cereals to feed to the stock – it's just that we do it differently.'

As for the efficiency of the horses, David is realistic: 'I won't deny that they are slower. But having said that, we get all the jobs done in season, so do we need to go any faster? Financially we couldn't convert now, but that's not the reason I keep on with the horses. If John's not able to carry on with the horses for whatever reason, I will certainly try to do so and Frances will support me in that. Hopefully Richard will too in later years – so long as farming remains viable.'

Like his father-in-law, David is happy to stay rooted to the farm right through the changing seasons. 'For Richard's sake we try and get three or four days a year off and go to the Lake District or somewhere like Beamish Museum. But apart from that I like to stay at home. The last real holiday I had was my honeymoon!

'On a farm like this there's always something to be done, even if it's just looking after the stock. And also I feel that, for all John's looked after the farm for many years, he's getting to the stage where I don't want to leave him with too much work. I know he's quite capable of it and will be for a good few years yet. But I still feel in the back of my mind that if something went wrong I would be happier if I was at home.'

Not that the two men don't differ from time to time. John has set ways of doing things. David, with fresh ideas, might suggest an alternative course of action. 'Occasionally we fall out, but it tends to be a quick flare-up and then it's forgotten. It's usually something quite small, and either one or the other will give in or we come to a compromise. But 99 per cent of the time we're happy and things go smoothly. If John and I didn't hit it off together, it wouldn't work on a place like this. It would make life very difficult, because you rely on each other such a lot.'

How the future will turn out is difficult for David to predict, but he knows that Frances will have a large part to play. 'Frances is heavily involved in the day-to-day running of the farm: feeding sheep, looking after sheep. She's worked a long time with the horses, and she knows a lot about them too.

'Richard is now getting to the age when we can send him to the top of the field if there's a ewe lambing and he'll look and see. He's not at the stage where he can bring her in yet, but he can come back and tell us. It saves us a journey every time.

'As far as the horses are concerned he is interested. He has a small Shetland pony and he would like to work with the heavy horses. Sometimes we let him hold the reins when he's with us. He's done a little bit of ploughing with his granddad, and he's shaping up well. But time will tell. The opportunity's there for him if he wishes to take it up.'

Norman Barber

Norman Barber is reliving his youth by helping out at Sillywrea. Now 73, he's gone back to working with horses and rekindled his love of the land – land he turned his back on 53 years ago.

Norman was brought up on a farm in Northumberland, the son of a farm worker. At 14 he joined his father, working with him in the fields, learning how to look after livestock and how to handle horses. The expression for a father-and-son combination was 'double hind' and farmers were keen on the arrangement because they got two workers while only having to provide one tied cottage. John Dodd says: 'I never knew Norman's father, but from all accounts he was a grand countryman and he gave Norman a good training.'

At 17, Norman had a spell as an assistant groom, looking after hunters at the stables of a local squire. This fed his desire to work with horses, but he missed the land, so he went back into farm work. Finally, though, the poor wages began to tell. At the age of 20, Norman left agriculture and started driving lorries.

For the next 45 years Norman worked for a transport company leading stone, gravel and concrete slabs from the local quarry. He hadn't entirely severed his links with farming, however. He had a part-time job as a relief dairyman, milking cows on a large farm whenever the cowman was off. Not surprisingly, Norman's fellow lorry drivers wouldn't let him forget his background. When CB radios began to find their way into cabs Norman got himself one. It was inevitable he should acquire the handle of 'Dairy Man'.

When he retired, Norman thought he'd lead a quiet life. But he soon became restless.

He took over as groundsman at the village sports field; home of the local cricket team. There was the outfield to cut with his gang mowers, the boundary to mark and wickets to lay out. After a game there were bowlers' footholds to fill in and batsmen's guard marks to level. But it wasn't enough.

One day Norman thought he'd go to Sillywrea and take some photographs of the horses. He fell into conversation with John and they got talking about the old days and how Norman had been raised among horses. Soon he was coming to lend a hand at busy times. 'You never forget what you've learned about horses,' he says. 'It all came back quite quickly.'

When John had a heart attack in 1995, Norman stepped into the breach, helping to muck out the cattle in winter and work on the land in spring. At haytime he was a constant visitor. 'I've always enjoyed the horses, ever since I could run after them,' he says. 'It's been a dream come true, the chance to work with them again after all these years.'

Clydesdales

Where the ploughland meets the heather
And earth from sky divides
Through the misty northern weather
Stepping two and two together
All fire and feather
Come the Clydes!

Will H. Ogilvie

They were lean, hairy and big-boned but their owners swore by them. In the north of England and Scotland in the 19th century and the early part of the 20th Clydesdales were the most popular work horses. As draught animals capable of sustained work they provided power at a time when it was needed by a country being propelled forwards by the industrial revolution.

Placid though they may be today, Clydesdales and their kindred breeds – Shire, Suffolk Punch and Percheron – have a warlike past. The ancestors of the horses used by John Dodd and David Wise were the chargers of old, giant beasts which carried warriors into battle during the wars of the middle ages. As one writer put it, our history is written on their backs.

The war horse, often described as the 'great horse', was bred to carry a knight clad in prodigious amounts of heavy armour. Protected by steel plate or chain mail it was driven full-tilt at the enemy, an instrument of destruction weighing considerably more than a ton. Opposing forces on foot would have quaked in terror at the sight of such a fearsome beast bearing down on them. In troops of armoured cavalry, the great horses and their riders became an essential part of an army's weaponry. In the Norman invasion of 1066 the English army, which had no cavalry, came face-to-face with William of Normandy's armoured knights, whose crashing waves overwhelmed the gallant Saxon infantry. The Norman horses were not huge by today's standards, measuring about 14 hands high, but the shock effect was more than enough to carry the day at Hastings.

The search for larger and larger war horses continued as the centuries rolled by. Breeders throughout Europe introduced new bloodlines to give their mounts more size and strength. As the 15th century drew towards a close, the massive European 'destrier', or charger, was expected to carry in tournament or battle almost 500lb of armour, as well as its noble knight. His steed was his proudest and most expensive possession, a status symbol as well as a beast of burden.

With the invention of gunpowder, and in particular the cavalry pistol, the invincibility of the war horse was threatened. A pistol ball could pierce any armour and bring down a horse whose steel protection might previously have warded off the blows of swords and axes. As a result, mounted soldiers switched to lighter horses which were more manoeuvrable.

Dispensed with by the military, heavy horses took on a new role in civilian life. In 1564 Queen Elizabeth I commissioned a travelling waggon so that she could make the journey from London to Warwick. It was pulled by six draught horses. Encouraged, the queen and her retinue began making visits to far-flung corners of the kingdom, transported by waggon trains drawn by 400 heavy horses. Only heavy horses could cope with the atrocious condition of roads at that time.

The development of collars and harness for work horses accelerated their introduction into agriculture. So too did the improvement of grassland to support these great beasts through the year. And as more farm machinery was invented, the need increased to find animals which were more intelligent and versatile than the ox.

Lanarkshire in the west of Scotland, where the River Clyde flows, is the area that saw the early development of Clydesdales. But it didn't take long for them to spread to other areas. In 1805 John Bailey and George Culley visited Northumberland in order to compile a report on the state of the county's agriculture. They noted that Northumberland farmers were beginning to use Clydesdale horses. 'These strong, hardy horses are remarkable good and true pullers, a restive horse being rarely found among them.'

As horse breeders sought to improve their native stock they turned to using stallions imported from Flanders. Farmers wanted weight and power in their work horses, coupled with longevity. But although originally bred for farming, Clydesdales were also used for street work in the mining and industrial areas of Scotland. They worked in large teams for the foundries and shipyards and were noted for their smart, brisk action, much quicker than that of the ponderous, bulky Shires which were the most popular heavy horses elsewhere in Britain.

A Clydesdale horse stands between 16 and 17 hands high (between 5 foot 3 and 5 foot 6) and weighs between 16 and 17 hundredweight. There are a variety of colourings. A bay with distinctive white markings on the face and dark forelegs and white hindshanks is considered an ideal combination. The exceptional wearing qualities of the Clydesdales' feet and legs are their most important feature. John Dodd reckons a good Clydesdale will last at least 20 years.

Until the advent of tractors on farms worldwide, Clydesdale horses were shipped in vast numbers to Australia and New Zealand, where there were many settlers of Scottish ancestry. Today some are still exported to the USA, where they're used in displays but rarely worked on the land.

There are usually five Clydesdale horses at Sillywrea. The oldest at the moment is Jock. 'He's the one with the white splash up the hip and oh, he's a nice stamp of a horse,' says John. 'Fifteen years old and as sound as a bell. He's a little bit under-sized but he's big enough for farm work. I bought him for £170 privately from the late Jim Addison, of Red House, at Great Orton just outside

Carlisle. He kept him for the winter and delivered him in the spring as a yearling. We don't buy many privately, but sometimes a horse breeder comes and says they've got something you might be interested in. We called him Jock after Jim's brother.'

David appreciates Jock's traits: 'He's a nice quiet lad. A good hard worker.'

Then there's Dick. 'By, how time flies,' says John. 'Dick will be 10 now, it seems only yesterday when he was a foal. He's a half brother to Jock. We called him Dick after my grandson, Richard. We got him as a foal for 250 guineas from the same farmer as Jock. He has a bit of a temper on him, so you have to watch him, but he's a good strong horse who will work all day.' David's opinion: 'Now he's a fiery boy. He likes to get a move on, so you need to keep a tighter rein on him.'

Davey is a full brother to Dick. 'He's nine years old. We named him Davey after my son-in-law. I liked him the first time I saw him at Jim Addison's farm. He was 325 guineas, which may seem a lot compared to the others, but they threw in some old harness and a cart as "luck" so I was happy with the deal.'

David says Davey is his favourite: 'Partly

because of his name, but also because he's the one I've done the most with. He went off to a horse-breaker for six weeks and I've done all the breaking work with him since then. He was very young and green when he came back, and I had to get him used to all the implements. He can be a bit tempery, but I like Davey. He gets on with the work but when, and if, you need him to stop in a hurry, he does.'

Sandy is the fourth member of the team. It's obvious where he got his name. 'I bought him at Wigton Horse Sale six years ago. He was 370 guineas, which was more than I'd normally pay, but I could see our David liked him. He's the first strawberry roan horse we've ever had. He's such a steady worker, and one of the quietest horses we've ever had.'

David says: 'He's the tallest of them all. He may be quiet, but he has his own character. For instance, he didn't use to like water. I had a lot of bother with him as a young horse, trying to get him to walk through puddles. Time and patience is what you need for a horse, and he's all right now.'

Robin is coming up to four now. He was bred by Sir Charles Kerruish, of Ballafoyle, Maughold, Isle of Man, and John paid 300 guineas for him at Wigton Horse Sale in October 1997. 'We had a horse called Robin who looked exactly the same and he was a good 'un so we called this one Robin too. He's really my favourite colour: red bay with three white legs and one black, and a nice-marked white face. He's not the height of Sandy, but at 17 hands he's a shade bigger than Jock or Dick.

'Robin's not quite as lazy as Sandy. He has a bit more life in him, but he was just as easy as Sandy to break in. We could possibly have done without him and bought a cheaper foal the following year, but it's all right being wise after the event. Everyone knows which horse to back when the race is won! Four horses are plenty really, but on the other hand if anything goes wrong, you need something in reserve, and it'll be another year before Robin is fully broken in.

'Meanwhile I can't speak too highly of him. He's a classic Clydesdale – with a lovely temperament.'

The number of heavy horses on farms in Britain reached its peak in 1914 when official statistics recorded almost 1.5 million. Even with the wholesale destruction of heavy horses on the battlefields of the First World War, where many were used to haul guns, there were still 1,386,000 on agricultural holdings in 1919. The real fall came after 1945. In the following 30 years heavy horse numbers plummeted from 480,000 to 5,000. 'An utter tragedy,' says John. 'Great animals, many of them. Sent to the knacker's yard in their thousands.'

No one can be directly blamed for the decline, but John says that the agricultural inventor Harry Ferguson has a lot to answer for. It was he who added the power take-off point and hydraulics to his little grey Ferguson tractors – features which earned them the ironic title of 'farm work horses' because they could do all the jobs that horses could do, and more. 'Oh, no doubt it was seen as progress,' says John. 'And tractors have got bigger and better ever since. But I feel that many things done in the name of progress just seem to spell the end of a way of life.'

Among the rural population, there's a strong affection for animals like the five Clydesdales at Sillywrea. But will farming in Britain ever go back to horses? John thinks not. 'We're too far down the road of mechanisation,' he says. 'I can't really see horses coming back. We've reached the point of no return.'

Spring

Ploughing

Daffodils lining the farm lane that leads to Sillywrea herald the arrival of spring. There's a shimmer of green on the hawthorn hedgerows and the larch trees in the surrounding woods sprout purple buds. Cock pheasants cough in the thickets. Moles are moving earth.

It ought to be a time of optimism. But John Dodd believes that winters are getting longer and wetter. Sometimes in the early part of a new year, he says, there's a false dawn. A warm spell in February lifts the spirits – only for them to be dashed by frosts in March.

'It's one thing the scientists have got right,' John says drily. 'The weather. They say it's getting worse and it is.

'I can remember lovely spring days when we used to take all the carpets out of the house to beat them. Spring cleaning time. Sometimes it might be a bit damp and you'd have to hang them over the clothes line before you went at them with a carpet beater. But often it was so dry you could beat them on the ground. Can you imagine that today? The springs we get are far too wet.'

Like most countrymen, though, John draws on a well of old sayings:

Of all the months in the year
A fine February's the one to fear

The meaning is clear. If it's fine in February the chances are it'll be wet for the rest of the spring. All the more reason to still have 'half your corn and half your straw' on Candlemas Day (2 February) because you just don't know what the rest of the winter will bring.

Far better, many country people feel, to suffer a wet February:

February fills the dyke
Black or white

This is a February when all the ditches are awash with snow or rain. In theory, that should be your share of bad weather for the year. But even if you survive the deluge of February, be cautious:

Ne'er cast a clout
'Ere May is out.

Another reference to the fickle nature of the weather – in other words, don't peel off that outer layer of clothing until May's over. There can always be late frosts.

Provided the weather is settled and the ground is reasonably dry, however, the end of winter and the early days of spring at Sillywrea present a welcome opportunity for David and John to plough fields of stubble left over from the previous year's barley crop. This land has had manure spread on it by hand, and ploughing will bury the manure and the stubble, while exposing the furrows to the cleansing and disintegrating effects of air, rain and frost.

Ploughing is a practice which goes back to the dawn of time, when digging sticks were the first implements to be used by primitive peoples seeking to improve the land in which they grew their crops. Until the latter part of the 18th century ploughs were made of wood, often shaped from a tree hardened by the smoke of gorse or bracken. Oxen provided the pulling power, teams of up to ten animals – sometimes assisted by horses – dragging crude wooden ploughs through the soil. One man drove the animals, another exerted his weight on the plough to keep its point in the ground, and a third guided it over the land. Following them came a group of men and women who broke up the clods with forks and mattocks (pickaxes).

An old ploughman's saying stems from the days of oxen as draught animals:

He who by the plough would thrive
Must either hold himself or drive

This meant that if a farmer was to benefit from using a plough to improve his land, he had to show he knew how to do it – by leading the oxen or holding the handles.

The ploughs used by John and David are the direct descendants of ploughs developed at the beginning of the 19th century. These implements transformed the art of ploughing, as a northern poet recognised at the time:

One man can now, with two good mares
Plough more in good March weather
Than four horses then, with cows and
    steers,
Man, lads and all together

The principal parts of the plough are the coulter, an angled knife with a sharpened edge which makes the first cut in the soil; the share or point (also known as the sock), which slices the soil horizontally, and the mouldboard, which turns the furrow. At one time, because of a superstition that too much iron might poison the land, only the parts of the plough in direct contact with the soil were made of iron, but as designs became more refined the frame and all the working parts were fashioned out of iron too.

The depth and width of a furrow can be regulated by changing the position of a short chain on the hake, a notched metal loop at the front of the plough, or by altering the position of a pin in the quadrant attached to the hake. The height of the two metal wheels at the front of the plough can also be raised or lowered, and the angle of the coulter adjusted. 'There are so many ways you can adjust the settings,' David says. 'People think these old ploughs are simple, but they are a lot more sophisticated than they look. Altering the height of the ploughwheel by just a quarter of an inch can make all the difference.

'Horse ploughing is something you learn

over a period of years. I've picked up a lot from John, just watching him or listening to him. Many factors can influence the way you plough. The condition of the land, a shower of rain which dampens the field, the way the two horses work together. Sometimes you can have one horse pulling harder than the other. Davey's like that. He's keen to work when you first start in the morning and if he's paired with Dick, who's a bit more easy-going, you might have to adjust the buck (quadrant) to compensate, otherwise you can end up with a narrow strip of unploughed land.'

With today's huge tractors and reversible ploughs capable of turning over five furrows at a time, ploughing has lost its finesse. Any tractor driver can go into a field, plough up and down and finish off the edges without thinking about it. Horsemen are different. They know there's a right way and a wrong way to plough a field.

'All fields vary in shape but you want to make sure you end up with the furrows meeting in the middle,' John says. 'So you have to pace out the land and mark it with sticks to show you where to plough.'

Over the years John has collected a number of ploughs but the one he uses most is a Ransome. Robert Ransome, the son of a Quaker schoolmaster from East Anglia, patented a method for tempering plough-shares in 1785 and in 1803 brought out his revolutionary self-sharpening plough. The firm he founded made horse ploughs until the Second World War.

A pair of Clydesdales working with an experienced ploughman can plough an acre a day. It's hard work. However finely tuned the plough may be, striking a large stone can jar the ploughman's arms and shoulders. When he's ploughing stony ground John always walks closer to the plough in case it hits a stone and the stilts (handles) deal him a blow to the ribs. He's lucky to be short and stocky. Bending over the stilts for long periods can be wearing for a tall man. And lifting the plough out of the furrow at the headland (the turning area at the end of the row) is physically demanding.

There's also a need for dexterity. One horse walks in the furrow and the other – usually the one which is keener to work – on the unploughed land. The ploughman has to wrap the reins controlling the two horses round his hands, as well as grasp the wooden handles of the plough to guide it through the earth. If the field is difficult to plough or the horses are misbehaving, the ploughman can skin his hand where the reins cut in. Of course, as with all the aspects of working with heavy horses, the old horsemen insisted there was a right way and a wrong way to hold the reins. 'By rights, you shouldn't wrap the reins around your hand, you should just grasp them,' says John. 'But I just wrap them round once and then, if a horse is going to bolt and you can't hold it, you just straighten your fingers and you don't get caught.'

And then there's the distance a ploughman walks: 10 to 12 miles every acre.

No wonder a ploughman's lunch is a hefty meal!

Nevertheless, David is rarely happier than when he's ploughing. 'It's the job I like the most,' he says. 'I love the steady pace of the horses and the sound of the harness clinking. You're more open to the elements, you feel the wind and the rain and the sun. And you're closer to nature, with the seagulls swooping behind you.

'At the end of the afternoon you can see what you've done, and if the conditions are right and you've made a nice true furrow and a good finish, well, you feel you've done a good day's work.'

In the years up to the Second World War,

when almost all farm work was carried out by horses, ploughing was an art to be judged by all. Ploughmen knew that any field close to a road would be scanned by neighbours passing by, and the comments would be caustic if the furrows weren't straight. Ploughing matches, still as strongly supported today as they were a century ago, sprang from this competitive spirit, with ploughmen striving for the perfect look: land lying in even furrows and glinting in the sunlight like corrugated iron sheeting after a shower of rain.

Lambing Time

A lamb lay motionless in the straw in the sheep shed. The mother hovered nearby, baa-ing loudly. John looked down at them, considering what to do. He reached into his coat and took out his pocket knife. Without pausing he slipped the blade under the lamb's skin. The animal had been stillborn, but John knew that if he acted quickly there was an opportunity to give another lamb a chance to live. Skilfully he stripped the thin, purled skin from the lamb's inert body, leaving holes for the feet and head. In a pen made of bales at the corner of the sheep shed was another small lamb rejected by its mother. John lifted it over and, ignoring its protests, dressed it in the dead lamb's skin. It wasn't a perfect fit but it would do. He now had to confine the baa-ing ewe to a pen in the shed and convince her that this was her lamb. Dressed in the lambskin it would have the right smell.

Once again, skills John had learned from his father and passed on to his daughter were coming into play. Lambing is a time of stress for flockmasters. A Northumbrian writer once observed: 'A sheep's main aim in life is to die before you want it to.' The same wit also described the spade as 'an all-purpose lambing tool', in a reference to how much time is spent burying lambs that never make it into this life. But, given freedom from disease and a prolonged spell of good weather, lambing can be a satisfying, if exhausting experience.

For the last couple of centuries the northern counties of England and Scotland's Border country have been renowned for the skill of their shepherds and the outstanding quality of their livestock. In 1866, 18 years after John's great grandfather bought Sillywrea, the Government carried out the most comprehensive census of agriculture that had ever been done in Great Britain. It showed that there were more than 22 million sheep on the nation's farms with, even then, high populations in Northumberland, Cumberland and Westmorland (now Cumbria), County Durham and Yorkshire. A census covering the same subject a century later showed that the national flock had grown larger, but the increase – to 28 million – was relatively small. It's only in the last 35 years that there has been an explosion in sheep numbers to almost 43 million.

The rise in the number of sheep at Silly-wrea has not kept pace with the national trend. While the size of the flock run by John, David and Frances has gone up slightly in recent years, to roughly 200 ewes, it is limited by the size of the farm. They can't keep vast numbers of animals, so they try to boost their income by targeting specialised markets.

Seventy of the ewes are Suffolks, a popular, chunky breed of sheep used throughout Britain to produce lamb for butchers' shops. Fifty of the Suffolks are bred pure (mated with Suffolks), the best ewe lambs being kept as flock replacements and the remainder sold fat. Most of the male offspring are sold as shearling (18-month-old) rams, which means they generate considerably more income than they would if simply sold as fat lambs.

A further 20 Suffolk ewes are mated to a Cheviot ram to produce lambs which will mature quickly and get better prices at fatstock sales. Then there are 90 Cheviot ewes, 35 bred pure and the rest mated to Suffolk rams. Again, the aim is to have lambs ready for market before the autumn glut when prices traditionally fall. The remainder of the flock are Cheviot ewe hoggs (female sheep aged six to 12 months) which are put to a ram of a comparatively new breed in the Britain, the Bleu de Maine.

All along, John and his family are hoping that better quality will result in better financial returns. But there is a downside. To catch the early markets, ewes are mated sooner than is usual and lambs start arriving at Sillywrea in February rather than March or April. It can mean a cold start for many tiny lambs and they tend to demand more attention than later-born animals. A lot of time is spent shuttling ewes and young lambs between the 'maternity ward' – the sheep shed – and an old orchard behind the farm house, where they spend the day in the open air – a healthier place to grow. Later, they stay out all the time in grass fields close to the farm. The animals still have to be checked constantly so it's easier to have them close at hand. In early May the sheep are moved to fields further away and the meadows where they had their lambs are 'closed off' so that the grass can grow for hay.

Farmers like John and David treat these fields just as gardeners treat their lawns: they're raked and rolled to encourage the grass to grow.

Among Sillywrea's assortment of old horse-drawn implements are two or three sets of chain harrows. These are ten-foot-wide contraptions made of linked loops of steel with pointed teeth jutting down on the underside. Light enough to be pulled by a single horse in chain harness but heavy enough to make their mark, they're used to drag out dead grass and moss, spread the remains of manure left unrotted in the field and level off molehills. No one wants molehills lurking in hayfields, because they blunt the knives of mowers when the time comes to cut the grass.

Like the chain harrows, rollers used to flatten grassland are pulled by a single horse with the horseman walking behind. Horse-drawn rollers were made of iron, steel or concrete. Sometimes hollow steel rollers were filled with water to give them extra weight. Sitting atop the steel frame was a box for stones too large for the machine to squash into the ground. John's Sellar roller, with its tubular metal shafts, was bought at the dispersal sale of Ashington Coal Company Farm back in the 1950s. But he has another, older roller which was bought by his father when John was a boy and is still going strong. True testament to the enduring qualities of old machines.

Horsemen don't always enjoy harrowing and rolling grass – especially when the weather's changeable. Sometimes in May great clouds well up from the west and heavy showers sweep over man and beast marooned in the field. There isn't enough time to 'loose out' (uncouple) the horse, so they have to wait there, steam rising from the horse's back, rain pattering on the driver's oilskins, until the downpour has passed. But mostly rolling and harrowing produces a sense of satisfaction. A glance back at the field on the way home and the sight of light- and dark-green stripes, as straight and even as any lawn, give a feeling of a job well done.

'I like all the seasons of the year, but spring is my favourite,' says David. 'There's a sense of renovation. Things are growing again: young lambs, young calves. The grass is starting to shoot up. Everything is being rejuvenated and that lifts you after the winter.'

Sowing Seed

On upland farms in the north of England pied wagtails are known as the 'seed birds'. Not because they eat seeds, but because having spent the winter in the warmer lowlands they return to the higher ground farming areas at the same time as farmers there are getting ready to sow seed in the spring.

Ploughed fields intended for barley are worked down to a fine tilth, and as soon as it's warm enough the seed drill is dragged from the implement shed and set ready to work. One way farmers used to judge if the soil was fit was to lower their trousers and test its temperature with their bare buttocks. John Dodd doesn't attempt anything so undignified. 'I just take a clod and nip it in my fist,' he says. 'You can tell from the way it crumbles whether it's ready.'

Tradition dictates the pattern of the

countryside calendar. 'My father used to say you should start to sow the corn by the first day of spring, March the 21st, if you wanted to make sure you had a good crop. I remember in 1947, the year of the great snow storm and the worst winter in living memory, we started to sow on the 16th of April and my father thought that was late. But these days we're struggling to get the land ready for planting in March. We just don't seem to get the dry springs we used to get.

'Deciding when to sow can be awkward. Sometimes you want to get on with it because the spring's advancing, but there's no point in hurrying things. If it's too damp the discs on the drill clog up. You just have to be patient.'

Whether it's a good sign or not, the pied wagtails are back at Sillywrea at the start of another season at the farm as David prepares to yoke Dick and Davey, the full brothers, into the seed drill. It's an American-made Massey-Harris, and it's one of the most youthful pieces of equipment on the farm. Belonging to the last generation of horse-drawn corn drills to be sold in Britain, it dates from the early 1940s, before horses gave way to tractors. But its ancestry can be traced back to Jethro Tull's revolutionary seed drill of 1701. It's said that Tull, a barrister who had a small farm and played the organ in a country church at weekends, was gazing idly at the organ pipes when it occurred to him that a mechanical seed drill could be based on their design. Until that time crops were broadcast by hand, labourers carrying seed boxes on straps round their shoulders and sowing the corn left and right with even sweeps of their arms. Tull got his local blacksmith to make a drill which brought precision to the practice. Forced by small brushes moving at the same speed as the drill's land wheels, seeds trickled from a box mounted on top of the horse-drawn machine on to a grooved cylinder which separated them one by one. From there they fell down pointed pipes into narrow gashes cut by coulters in the soil. The result was that the seed grew in neat rows.

Much the same principle governs the operation of John and David's 18-row Massey-Ferguson planter, even though 300 years have passed since Tull had his inspiration during a church service. Naturally, there have been improvements on the original – including the introduction of metal discs which cover over the seed after it has fallen from the pipes, and handles which enable the driver to move the drill in and out of gear, so that sowing pauses while the horses turn on the headlands. But in other respects, what David is driving is very much the same as the 18th-century original.

In the 19th century seed drills were manufactured in large numbers in different parts of the country, and some could be very expensive. In 1894 a Lincoln firm launched a new 16-row drill costing £30. John chuckles at the price. 'I bought mine for £8 at a farm sale in the 1950s,' he says. 'Mind, it's needed one or two parts. Six of the tubes perished. They cost me £18 each to renew, which made the spare parts £100 more than the cost of the drill itself.'

A two-horse drill like John's can sow an acre of corn in an hour. The person walking behind the machine has to concentrate all the time. The main thing is to watch the wheelmarks left by the previous pass and make sure seed is flowing from all the pipes. After all, it's not just the ploughing that country people look critically at. They're sure to spot the gaps in the rows if your drill's not been working properly!

The Farrier

Early spring brings another regular visitor, the have-anvil-will-travel farrier. When all farms kept heavy horses, a trip to the blacksmith's was an event in itself that could take half a day by the time you'd led or rode the horse there and back. Sometimes you'd take two horses. And if someone else in the neighbourhood had the same idea – wet days in summer were favourite times to have feet checked – it could take the whole day. The pace of life was easier and blacksmiths' shops were a place where farm hands and retired farmers liked to pass the time, their faces lit red by the glow of the coal as they gathered round the forge fire. Every village or hamlet had its own blacksmith's ringing out with the sound of hammer on metal and a boy working the bellows with a long wooden handle.

From Sillywrea, John could choose from five different blacksmiths, all within a five-mile radius of the farm. Some were notoriously bad-tempered, as if working with big horses tested their patience. It probably did.

117

Now in the 21st century the farrier comes to the farm, all his tools, his anvil and even his furnace stashed in the back of a van.

Most of John's horses don't need shoeing. They work on the fields and travel from one side of the farm to the other by bridle path. There isn't much road on the farm to wear their feet down. 'We haven't shod our horses for about 30 years, but when we did we used to reckon on shoes lasting about 3 months,' John says.

Unusually, David and John have agreed to look after a horse for an acquaintance and it needs shoeing. John explains, 'The horse used to pull a bus for tourists visiting Holy Island off the coast of Northumberland. He gets footsore on his front feet so we have to have him shod every ten weeks. That's when we give Simon Heslop a ring. He's a young chap who served his time with a blacksmith at Baty's in Hexham, and rather than take a shop he has a van. He goes round the country and has a tremendous amount of trade, a lot of hunting horses and ponies.

The horse is also called Simon. He's a 17-hand-high Clydesdale bay gelding with a white blaze on his face and white legs. Simon Heslop the farrier has strapped on his leather apron and is getting his blacksmith's

118

tools out of the van as David leads the horse across the yard. The farrier takes the front foot between his knees and goes to work with the parer, nipping great chunks off the hoof and then placing the foot on a metal stool and completing the pedicure with a rasp. Sweat dripping from his forehead as he works, he admits it's hard work – and potentially dangerous. 'How do I work?' he says. 'With caution. It all depends on the person who's holding the horse's head. You put your trust in him. They're big horses and you try and work fast. But it still takes time, twice as long as it takes to shoe a hunter.'

Simon has brought a homemade tool-holder with him. Poking out of its compartments are a selection of tools, many of which he's made himself. He turns on the Calor Gas forge and flings a match into its mouth. It ignites with a *whoosh*, and within minutes the two shoes heating up in it are red hot. Horseshoes have to fit exactly. Simon takes one of the shoes and hammers it into shape on the anvil before placing it lightly on the upturned hoof; smoke rises from the scorched horn. He will reheat the shoe and make minor adjustments to it before nailing it in place and filing down any rough edges.

'It's a joy coming to Sillywrea. There are

other people who keep Clydesdales as a hobby but, you know, these horses aren't pets, they're big strong animals and sometimes you can have a bit of fun with them,' he says drily. 'Here, because they're used to work, they're easier for a farrier like me. Work keeps them quiet. John's worked with horses all his life and when he buys a yearling in October he always looks for a good stamp of horse with good feet and strong bone. He teaches them manners and it's just a joy to work with them, because they're so easy and so well behaved.'

Feeding Sheep

John decides it's time to take a cartload of mangolds out to ewes and lambs in the fields. Sheltering in the shed, with its two six-foot-long shafts pointing skywards, is a cart used for many of the jobs at Sillywrea. Like all the implements at the farm, it has a long and evocative link with the past.

Two hundred and fifty years ago it was only the well-to-do landowners and yeoman farmers who could afford carts, and in many places farm crops like hay and corn were transported by wooden horse-drawn sleds. Early farm carts were crude affairs with wheels made of three pieces of wood held in place by wooden pins. They were attached to an axle which turned laboriously under the frame of the cart, producing excruciating squeals as one wooden surface ground against another. It was said, half seriously, in those days that a cow's horn filled with fat for lubricating the axle was as essential an accessory for a waggon man as a stick to prod the oxen.

Wheelwrights changed all that. By the middle of the 19th century they were making carts of a much improved design. The main difference was that the wheels turned on the axle and not with it. And the new, iron-clad wheels extended the life of the cart considerably.

The making of the cart wheel was a skill honed by years of practice. The hubs were usually turned from well seasoned elm. The spokes were always of oak, usually riven rather than sawn to maintain the strength of the grain. And the felloes (sections of the rim) were ash, grown curved if possible. Hooping the wheel with an iron 'tyre' was an art. The tyre had to be heated in a blacksmith's fire until it glowed red hot, picked up by two men using tongs and slipped over the wheel, which rested on a circular metal tyring platform. After a flurry of hammering and levering with tyre 'dogs', the smoking metal was quenched with cold water so that it contracted and fitted snugly round the felloes. Accuracy was essential. If the tyre was too big it would fail to clamp the wheel and would run off the rim in no time at all. If it was too small it would distort the wheel and possibly break it.

It took four days to make a pair of cartwheels, but those made by the most experienced wheelwrights could last for half a century.

Wheelwrights developed an instinctive feel for wood. They would search out copses and woodlands and buy trees as they stood for future use. On their travels they would make a mental note of ash trees growing in hedgerows which had natural curves or 'crooks'. They would buy the tree, fell it and leave it by the roadside for two years or more until the wood was properly hardened by time.

In many places the wheelwright was also the village wainwright who made waggons for carrying heavy loads. Every area had its own variations in cart design.

Unlike the wooden-wheeled vehicles of old, John's 'Scotch' cart has metal wheels and rubber tyres. It's a comparative youngster in the history of horse-drawn equipment. Nevertheless, it's had an astonishingly long life of hard daily graft and it's a tribute to its makers – and the care taken by three generations of the Dodd family – that it's still going strong. Bought by John's father at the Royal Highland Show at Melrose in the Scottish Borders in 1936, it was made by the well-known firm of Jacks, which was based at Maybole in Ayrshire on Scotland's west coast. 'They were great manufacturers and it's been a grand cart,' John says. 'It's been a loyal servant to us. But nothing lasts for ever when it's used every day, and after nearly 60 years of work it was looking a bit worse for wear. So David and I set to and renovated it. And we gave it a good lick of paint.' The colours are traditional to farms in south-west Northumberland: red shafts and a green body, with red 'overings' (additional boards slotted on top of the sides and front which increase the capacity of the cart). Splattered with mud after a wet winter, the cart's not as colourful as it was when it had just been restored. But it still looks well.

John backs Jock into the shafts of his Scotch cart. A long metal staple on top of each shaft holds a short chain, and this is attached to the tug hooks on the horse's collar. 'Gee up, Jock,' commands the farmer, and his horse lumbers forwards, hauling the empty cart across the yard. They pass through a metal gate to the field in front of the farm house, where mangolds are stored in a clamp covered with straw and bracken to protect them from the winter frosts. John reverses the horse to the open end of the heap. 'Back, back! Back, Jock!' he says. 'Whoa!' He ties the reins to the cart, just in case the horse takes it into his head to go for a wander. But Jock's too well-trained. He waits patiently as John starts to load the orange globes. Using a 'graipe' (four-pronged fork), he spears two mangolds at a time and tosses them into the cart. In no time at all, it's full. Off across the emerald-green meadow and through two gates they plod to join a flock of Suffolk ewes and lambs half a mile away from the farm. These animals have just been shifted from hayfields, where the grass is better, to an upland pasture where the sward doesn't provide as much nutrition. The mangolds give a boost to their diet and tide them over the transition.

A cacophony of bleating greets horse and cart. John removes the tail board from its hinges and, clasping the reins, climbs up among the mangolds to backheel them off the rear of the cart one by one as Jock moves slowly forwards. There's a loud and contented crunching sound as the sheep sink their teeth into the row of succulent roots. They certainly appreciate a springtime treat.

Mangolds are also known as mangel worzels. They're a turnip-like vegetable which resemble fodder beet. John's always had a liking for this versatile crop. 'If it's bad weather and we've brought the ewes inside there's no fear of the milk going off them if they get a mangold or two. And there's another situation where they're useful. Sheep lambing outside always feed with their backs to the wind and they can drift away to the exposed side of a field leaving their lambs hungry. What we do is take the horse and cart and leave a line of mangolds along the leeward side of a wall so that both ewes and lambs will eat there out of the wind.'

When the wind is in the east
'Tis neither good for man nor beast.
When the wind is in the west
Then the wind is at its best.

Horse Breaking

For John, 26 October 1995 was a special day. 'We were standing at the ringside at Wigton Horse Sale when they brought in a strawberry roan colt foal. We'd never had a strawberry roan before and maybe if it had been me on my own I wouldn't have gone after him. It's not a colour I'd choose. But I could see David liked the look of him so we bought him. He cost 370 guineas. It was a bit too much by my standards, but you forget all about that when you see the way he's turned out.'

They called the foal Sandy. And from the day he arrived at Sillywrea, John and David knew they'd got themselves a really special horse. Not a great looker perhaps. His youthful gawkiness drew some mildly critical comments from John. But for calmness of temperament Sandy has few equals.

When every farm relied on heavy horses many farmers bred their own. A farm might keep four horses: two geldings for work and two mares for work and for breeding. It didn't make economic sense for the farm to maintain a stallion, so a hire trade developed. These magnificent animals were walked by their owner or a groom from farm to farm and mated with mares that were in season. Seventy years ago, it cost £5 to have a mare served and a further £5 when she 'held' – proved to be in foal. In Scotland, the Clydesdale horse heartland, hiring societies were set up as long ago as 1837 in order to spread the best bloodlines and improve the breed. 'Aye,' recalls John. 'It was a great sight, a stallion arriving at the farm and the mares in the field running along the other side of the fence, snorting at him as he came down the lane with the groom. It was part of the farming calendar in those days. It was one of the signs of summer. My father liked horses and he bred a lot of foals, but for working horses I've always found it was cheaper to go and buy one and then break it in myself.'

Foals purchased by John spend the first two years running free. John believes they're better when they have another young horse as a companion, and he has an arrangement with John Cleasby, of Barton Church Farm, Tirril, who also likes to keep a Clydesdale foal or two. After spending their first winter and half the next year at Sillywrea, John's foals go to

Barton Church, where they can graze lush lowland fields until they're rising three and ready to break, which is usually in January.

'Company's a good thing. They do better when they're together because they're jealous of each other – competitive – and for some reason they eat better when they're like that. If you have one on its own it can sometimes turn a little bit pokey with its food. The whole aim is to get them to stay on a good plane of nutrition as they grow.'

During their first winter, the foals remain in the stable at night and go out during the day – provided the weather isn't too severe. 'It's a grand way of getting them used to being handled because we always catch them with halters. We never drive them in loose.'

John studies his horses closely from the day they arrive back at the farm. He wants to understand how they tick so that he can be prepared for training them. Watching them out in the fields, at rest and when they feed provides him with important pointers about their characters, as does the way they move and how they react to a range of different situations. Years of experience have taught him what kind of equine traits he might expect in a newcomer. 'No two horses are alike,' he says. 'But from the very start I knew through watching Sandy that there was a quiet calmness about him, and that's a quality you want to keep.'

The expression 'breaking a horse' may sound brutal. 'Training' would be a more accurate term. And ever since these wild herd animals were first domesticated, man has been developing techniques to get them to do what he wants.

'Every horse breaker has their own ways when they start with a young horse,' John says. 'Some say it's better to tackle them straight off the fells and then you get all the fight over at once. Myself, I like to handle the foals as they're growing up, and every morning when I go and look round the cattle I give them a pat and a stroke. It pays to keep slipping the halter on them, so they become used to the touch of the rope. I think it's best to handle them as much as you can. Handle them and talk to them. It saves a lot of trouble when it comes to breaking them.'

Having control over a horse depends on making sure it's got a 'good mouth'. It has to be encouraged to accept the bit as a natural part of its mouth, learning to swallow and produce saliva with it between its teeth. This is done by leaving the mouthing bit in a young horse's mouth for short periods. The mouthing bit has small 'keys' attached to it and they encourage the horse to work on the bit with their jaws. Getting a young horse used to the bit takes time and patience. It's important not to alarm the horse and destroy its confidence. If the bit is too high, it will damage the bars of the mouth. If it's too low, the horse may start putting its tongue over it, which is difficult to cure. When the time came to introduce Sandy to the mouthing bit he behaved in exemplary fashion and quickly became accustomed to it.

'The greatest thing about a young horse is getting it to have a good mouth, that is, a tender mouth. It sounds a little bit Irish, but the secret is to get the mouth hardened up and still remain a little bit tender. Never make their mouths bleed, because it's just like a callus on your hand. Every time it heals it grows thicker. If you skin their mouth when you're breaking them in, they'll have a tough mouth and you won't have any control over them. They're really creatures of habit. So long as they start doing a job right they'll do that job right all their lives. It's a funny thing, you can spend days teaching them something good, but they can learn something bad in half a minute. It's like a collie dog: you can take it out into the field and it can do everything perfectly, but if it makes a mistake you can be absolutely sure that it'll make the same mistake next day unless you correct it at once. And a horse is just the same. Bad habits are hard to change.'

An essential item of equipment in the early stages of horse breaking is what's known in northern England and the Borders as the 'muzzerole' but elsewhere is called the 'cavesson'. This is a kind of bridle with a well-padded noseband onto which is set a metal plate with three swivelling metal rings. To one of these rings can be attached a leading rein. This gives the trainer complete control over the horse.

In the early months of the year there are many routine chores to be done on a live-stock farm like Sillywrea. Feeding cattle and cleaning them out takes up a large portion of the shortened winter days. But there's still time to continue Sandy's training. He's two-and-a-half years old. The next stage is about to start.

To begin with, he's brought in from the fields and put in a loose box in the stable wearing a breaking harness to get him used to how it feels. The various parts of the breaking harness are designed to limit some of his movements while at the same time allowing him the freedom to walk and trot. Bearing reins are connected to the bit to prevent the young horse from dropping his head too low; a martingale hinders him from getting his head too high; and a tail cripple stops him from pulling the girth too far forward.

In early April, David takes him walking on the country roads near the farm. Sandy is still wearing the cavesson and breaking harness to ensure that David has control as he walks beside him, but the horse shows few signs of nervousness. 'We're trying to get him used to the traffic,' John explains. 'Not that we have a lot of traffic round here, but young drivers don't seem to understand horses any more and they certainly don't show the same respect that they used to. They seem to think these are just quiet ponies or brewery horses used to traffic in the town. And it's not just cars and lorries. A cycling club going swishing past can upset a young horse. So can a motor bike. Horses seem to be either really frightened in traffic, or very calm. And if they're really frightened, my, it's a hard job settling them down. But David's been getting on well with Sandy. He can walk better with him than I can. He's younger and stronger.'

Farmer and horse leave the farm and

follow a road which wanders northwards among fields bordered by stone walls and fences. Along the roadside dense thickets of blackthorn are covered with a mist of sharp-smelling white blossom. Celandines gleam yellow in the grass. A lane branches off to the left, leading down to a peat-stained river which is crossed by a narrow suspension bridge. Dippers nest in the stone cliffs above the water. Beyond the bridge lies a woodland where wood sorrel, red campion and bluebells will form a multi-coloured carpet in a few weeks' time. David turns Sandy and walks him back up the hill. 'You try and vary the route so that he gets used to different sights and sounds, be it a dog barking or a pheasant flying across the road in front of him, as well as the noise of cars driving by. But he's shaping up well. We'll do more road work with him on long reins to get him used to being controlled from behind as well as being led from the side.'

John is in the farm yard outside the stable door. He's hitched Sandy to a rail next to the water trough and the horse is drinking deeply John moves quietly round him, putting on the breaking harness. Firm commands ring out in the stillness of the yard: 'Come here!

Get off, man! Stand still! Enough!' as John patiently fits girth and reins. It's part of the process of showing who's in charge. John's voice sounds gruff and fierce, but he pats the horse affectionately as he unties him. He leads him across the cobbled yard, the clip clop of hooves echoing from the surrounding buildings. They go through a metal gate which clanks noisily. It's the kind of sound that could jangle the nerves of a young horse but Sandy shows no sign of being alarmed. They amble out to the paddock in front of the farm house. The next crucial stage in Sandy's training is about to begin.

This is lungeing – sending him round in a circle on the end of a 20-foot rope controlled by John, ringmaster-fashion, in the centre. The horse is sent first one way until the horsebreaker shouts, 'Whoa!' and he stops. Then he starts again, John shouting, 'Get on!' and, 'C'mon boy gee up!' and clicking his mouth as the horse circles him. After a while he's sent in the opposite direction. At one stage John goes and waves his cap at Sandy trying to distract him, but he ignores it. Even when John waves the rope, lasso style, it doesn't unnerve the young horse. Two short coils of rope hang from either side of the girth. They seem to serve no particular purpose, but as the horse trots round they bounce and flap against his flanks. Once again, he's being taught to accept the strange feeling of being brushed by unusual objects.

'Lungeing achieves a number of things,' John explains. 'It makes them obedient. They have to stop when you tell them. And it helps to tire them out. If they get above themselves, let them trot round while you stand in the middle. It'll settle them down. And lastly it's to get them more used to wearing harness. As they trot round they can hear the jingle of the harness and feel it against their sides.

'Sandy's full of spirit and full of life, but he hasn't shown any badness yet. We had him nice and fit and full of corn when we first started to lunge him, and that day he certainly was full of fight. The great thing is to get that fight out of them when you're breaking them in and not after they're yoked to a cart or a plough.'

The next test for Sandy will come when he is lunged in plough harness which is heavier and even noisier. Week by week, he's becoming more and more used to the life of work that lies ahead of him.

The stable at Sillywrea has changed little in over 100 years. You enter by a door cut in half, as all self-respecting stable doors should be. On one side, lit by windows, there are three stalls and a loosebox, each with its trough and manger. Built to hold heavy horses, they are wide and deep. On the opposite side, rows of hooks hold harness of various sorts. The animals are fed three times a day, groomed regularly and mucked out morning and evening. Brushes lean against the wall. The atmosphere is cosy. Even on the coldest night of winter the heat from the horses keeps the stable warm.

John is preparing for the next stage in Sandy's development. Pulling a cart will be one of the commonest jobs the horse will do, so it's time to try to accustom him to the claustrophobic feeling of having cart shafts on either side of his body. To the uninitiated, the most obvious way might seem to be to back the young horse into a cart and see what happens. But John doesn't want to leave anything to chance. He knows that might frighten a horse so much that it will never go near a cart again. All his careful work would be wasted. So he's devised a method which is probably unique.

Shafts are straight or slightly curved poles attached at one end to an implement or a vehicle and to a horse's harness fittings at the other. John has acquired two old single shafts and suspended them loosely on ropes on either side of a stall in the stable, the ends pointing outwards. These will be the first 'shafts' that Sandy will be tied to. It takes time to get the height right: John adjusts the ropes many times until he's satisfied.

Next he harnesses the horse, which is waiting quietly in the adjoining stall. First to go on is the draught collar, slipped on upside down to get it over Sandy's head and ears and turned the right way up once it's on his neck. It's a moment which horsemen down the years have savoured: the start of a new day's work. Heavy horse collars come in different sizes and must be a perfect fit to avoid neck sores. John has a good selection and he finds one which is just right for his youngster. Nestling against the front of the collar are two curved bars called hames, held in place by chains at the bottom and a strap at the top. Power is transferred through the collar and tug hooks on the hames to chains or shafts connected to an implement.

Horsemen like John question claims that a heavy horse's strength comes mainly from its shoulders. He asks: 'Does a horse push a cart or pull it? I always contend that the strength actually comes from the hindquarters which propel the body forward into the collar. That's why you choose a foal with good hips and powerful thighs. It will push hard against the collar.'

Sandy is still only half broken and control over him must be firm, so the 'muzzerole' is fitted to his head as it was during the leading and lungeing phases.

Then comes the bulky cart saddle, placed in the slight hollow of his back between the loins and withers. Like the collar, it's well padded. A wide metal groove runs over the top to take a chain linking the shafts on either side of the animal. The saddle is secured on the underside of the horse by a girth.

Lastly John lifts the britching (breeching) off its hook and places it over the horse's hindquarters. Vertical hip and loin straps support the breeching's wide leather straps that help a horse when it's backing, or hold its load in check on a steep slope.

Clad in his unfamiliar harness with its bulky, constricting straps, Sandy could quite justifiably feel threatened. But as he finishes fitting the harness John continues to talk quietly to the horse, encouraging him and patting him so as to keep him calm. Leaning and pushing against the giant horse's breast, John coaxes him to reverse into the stall where the shafts are waiting with gentle commands: 'Back! Back, Sandy back! That's a good lad.' For horses, going backwards is unnatural – they would rather see where they're going. But Sandy seems to trust his master and shuffles back until his head is in line with the end of the stall.

'You must start quietly with a young horse,' John admonishes. 'You have them for a long time after you've broken them in so you may as well take some pains at the start.'

Very gingerly, John starts to attach the 'shafts' to the harness and the collar, watching Sandy closely and talking quietly to him as he works. The horse seems to accept what's happening to him. Very occasionally he tenses and his eyes roll, but on the whole he stands still, even when John begins to move the shafts to and fro to simulate the movements Sandy would feel when pulling a cart. Extra lengths of chain are hung on to the harness and shaken so that they jingle loudly, but this doesn't disturb Sandy's serenity. John pats and strokes him con-tinuously, reassuring him. 'There's a grand lad,' he says. 'There's a grand lad.'

How unusual is this part of John's training system? 'No one ever told me this was the way to get horses used to working in shafts,' he says. 'I just thought it up for myself. It's not the same as being yoked in an implement but they do get used to the feel of the shafts and the rattling of the harness. Other horse breakers have other tricks but this has always worked for me. And up to now, this is the quietest young horse I've ever worked with.'

It will be a few months before John and David will try backing Sandy into the shafts of a real cart. He's got other things to learn first. Wearing chain harness and pulling a light implement is the next stage in his training. The routine is the same. Using a special 'ploughman's knot' taught to John by his father and passed on by him to his son-in-law, the reins are tied to the bit, as they usually are, and threaded through loops in the collar so that they stretch back to the driver. Trace chains leading back from the collar are fastened to two hooks on the front of a swingletree (spreader), a tubular iron bar with a single hook at the back onto which an implement is normally attached. To begin with, Sandy is taken out to a field and walked around, simply pulling the bar on its own until it's reckoned he's used to the sound and feel of it bumping and swishing in the grass behind him. The horseman is behind, holding the reins. The other man walks beside him. From pulling a single bar he progresses to pulling a heavy log. Once again, it feels different, because the piece of wood jerks and rolls in a disconcerting way. Then Sandy is yoked to a set of chain harrows. It's simple work, walking up and down a grass field in early summer with skylarks singing overhead, but it's all part of growing up. He's getting used to the feel of the harrows and the chinking noise they make as they bounce along.

For many farm tasks, heavy horses work in pairs. This is something else Sandy will have to get used to. John and David tie him loosely to one of their other horses and walk them up and down side by side. Then they yoke them up together to a cultivator. The team drags the machine through the soil of a ploughed field – and another skill has been learned by the young horse.

For a horse used to the tranquillity of the countryside, the next part of Sandy's tuition is a shock. He's about to find out what it's like pulling the noisiest and most awkward of farm machines, the grass cutter. Two horses lined up on either side of a draught pole haul mowers like these which are used every summer at Sillywrea. For a young horse like Sandy, it's a daunting experience. John admits: 'I often think it's a bigger trial to them than putting them in a cart. In the old days, when everyone had horses, it was always a worry when someone bought a work horse whether it would go in the mowing machine. It's a big test.'

To avoid problems at the start of haytime, when there's a big need to get on with grass cutting, David and John try and get Sandy used to the mower – by making him 'cut grass' in the cobbled yard back at the farm well before haytime begins. This dry run will prove how ready he is to tackle the real thing. The session takes place at the end of a day when the young horse has been working hard pulling cultivation equipment in an arable field. He's tired – and less likely to object.

'Some horse breakers like to do something like this out in a field where there's more space if they break loose,' John says. 'But I read a book called *A Lifetime with Ponies* by the late Roy Charlton, who lived not far from here, at The Linnels in Hexhamshire, and he said he always preferred to break in a horse in a confined space, because there was far less chance of panicking if it was surrounded by buildings. Since then I've always taken his advice. We're lucky here: we have a big yard we can rattle them round in. And touch wood, up to now it's worked. I must have had 40 horses in this situation. One night it was like a rodeo. The horse I was training was bucking and rearing all over the yard. But it settled down in the end. I've only had two that steadfastly refused to go in the mowing machine.'

Is John confident? 'I don't want to boast the luck out of him, but up to now Sandy's been fine. So, fingers crossed, he should pass the test.'

John and David clip the chains on to the front of the mower and buckle the pole to the underside of the horses' collars. In the field, the driver rides behind the horses on a scat, but John's not going to risk that in the farmyard. Certainly not at the outset. If Sandy bolted he'd be in trouble. So he sets off walking behind the team with the harness chains jangling and the metal wheels of the mower clattering on the cobbles. Round and round the yard they go, clockwise and anti-clockwise, until John judges that his young horse is safe to go in the field and cut grass along with the other horses. As he draws to a halt, John is clearly pleased: 'He was a little nervous, I could tell that. The pole touched his leg when we turned the first corner and he jumped a little and switched his tail, but that was all. For his first time with a mowing machine he was exceptional.'

A week later the grass is ready to cut for hay and Sandy is to pull a mowing machine in earnest for the first time. The tactics are the same. He's given a day's hard work preparing the land for turnips. After tea he's hitched to the mowing machine and driven round the farmyard two or three times just to make sure he's safe. Then, with the shadows lengthening in the setting sun, he's taken out to the field with Jock to cut his first swathe. He's reached another level of maturity.

High summer may be the season for making hay at Sillywrea, but other crops are growing apace and they need looking after too. A warm evening in August finds John and Sandy working in the turnip field. Their task: scuffling (weeding) turnips.

The rows of turnips, sown by Norman a couple of months ago, are ramrod straight. In July they were singled by David, Norman and John. They worked in line with swan's neck hoes, knocking out seedlings and leaving one every seven inches with space to grow. To catch a glimpse of them in the field was like watching an old film: no one else in the country still hoes turnips by hand.

For John, it brings back memories of a time when there was a ready source of labour from across the Irish Sea. 'Before and after the war we had Irishmen working here. They came to hoe turnips and do other work. They were fine fellows. They lived as cheaply as they could, worked hard, and sent the money they earned home to their families.'

Among local farm workers there were sometimes feelings of jealousy towards the itinerant labourers, mainly because the Irishmen were paid by the week or the day and the rates they negotiated were much higher than those earned by local farm hands. But the travelling workers were on a piece rate, so they had to do the work as quickly as possible. Often they would hoe turnips in the morning, sleep through the heat of the day and return to the fields in late afternoon to work until dusk. The turnip plants always stood up better in the cool of the day and were easier to hoe.

'Hoeing turnips, well, they were absolutely marvellous. Fast and accurate. We used to pay them by the chain (22 yards).'

Of course, measuring out the field wasn't a precise art. One farm not too far from Silly-wrea had steeply sloping fields which had been neatly planted with rows of turnips. The owner went out to inspect the crop with a visiting Irish worker who'd offered to hoe the field. Striding down the slope of the field, the farmer reckoned it was only so many chains from end to end. But the Irishman, puffing uphill with shorter steps, argued vehemently that the field was much longer than that! Eventually a compromise was reached.

John concedes: 'You sometimes had a bit of bother making a bargain with them, it's true. But once a bargain was made, they would never go back on it. They were as honest as the day is long.'

They were also shrewd. Having inspected a field of turnips belonging to a farmer in John's district, an Irish labourer agreed a price of 3d (just over a decimal penny) per 100 yards for hoeing them. Next morning, the Irishman was in the field at dawn. He'd realised that it was easily worked land and that the turnips were sown nice and thin, so it would be a quicker-than-usual job. He knew too that the farmer, realising the same thing, might go back on his word. So he made sure he would keep the man to the agreement – by being in the field at daybreak and making a start on every drill.

On many places the casual Irish workers

had to sleep in the hay barn and wash at a pump in the yard. But at Sillywrea, they stayed in the house and were well looked after. 'I learned a tremendous amount from working with them,' John says. 'They were the best mates ever I worked with in my life. They always said, start away with the job steady and get faster as you go, never start away in a rush or you sicken yourself. They're retired now, those Irish lads, but we keep in touch. It's more than 40 years since they worked here on the turnips but they still send us an Irish farming paper every month and we send them copies of the *Hexham Courant*.'

Singling crops like turnips gives them a good start. But controlling the weeds that spring up between rows is also essential. Whereas modern farmers spray selective weedkillers on their root crops, John and David stick to traditional methods at Sillywrea. The 'scuffler' used by them is a horse hoe made by a company called Pollock and bought by John during the war from Oliver and Snowden, a firm of agricultural merchants which was based in Haltwhistle, a small town 5 miles away. Like all their implements, it can trace its lineage a long way back – in the case of the 'scuffler' to the beginning of the 18th century when Jethro

Tull launched his seed drill. His drill may have been a breakthrough in terms of sowing seeds along precise lines, but Tull considered drilling to be secondary to hoeing. After all, if the turnip crop is swamped by weeds, why spend so much effort on preparing the soil in the first place?

Big though they are, the turnips in John's field are struggling to compete. There's been a prolonged spell of wet weather and chickweed is doing its best to strangle the crop, ably abetted by fat hen and redshank. They're all arable weeds which spring up every year wherever the ground's been disturbed. It's a challenge that Sandy and the scuffler will meet head on.

It's more good training for the young horse. The 'hake' (metal loop) at the front of the scuffler is attached to a swingletree (spreader) connected to trace chains leading back from Sandy's collar. Like most horse-drawn hoes, John's has a small wheel to support the fore end of the frame. The setting of the machine can be adjusted according to the width of the rows. Here they are 28 inches apart and the scuffler has been widened to cope. In John's skilful hands the job doesn't look unduly hard. Sandy daintily picks his way between the rows, his huge hooves somehow avoiding the turnips as he lumbers on-wards. The six arrow-head points on the tines disturb the roots of the weeds and they are left behind to wither. In the case of the chick-weed, the scuffler drags it out in handfuls.

The shiny leaves of the turnips glisten in evening sunlight slanting in from the west as John and his horse work up and down the rows. The only sound is the grating noise of metal on stone as the hoe blades meet the occasional obstacle in the soil. The machine may be 60 years old but it's wearing well.

Overhead, rooks caw as they start to fly back to their roost at the farm. Many countrymen use these birds as a way of telling what the weather will be. If they fly straight back to their nests the weather will stay warm and calm, it's said. But if they zigzag back, unsettled weather is on the way.

Looking back at the end of a row, John pronounces himself pleased. 'It's a good machine for grubbing out the weeds and Sandy's making a grand job of it. He's following the rows and never putting a foot wrong. And he's coming in at the ends of the rows just like an old-timer. He's marvellous altogether. I've never had one like him. He's a real "old man's horse" – the quietest I've had anything to do with.

'He'll work eight or 10 hours a day now, without any bother. And we should get 17 years' work out of him. He's three now and he should last until he's 20. That's why it pays to spend a lot of time on breaking him.'

What's the life expectancy of a heavy horse? 'Rule of thumb, the bigger the horse, the shorter the life. Some of those Shetland ponies will live until they're well over 30 but Clydesdales won't live quite as long, usually 20 to 25 years.'

A month later the moment arrives to continue Sandy's apprenticeship as a work horse. It's late afternoon on an early autumn day. A light wind fans a field of barley and swallows twitter on the telephone wires. In Far Pasture stands a roller. Sandy is going to be fastened between shafts for the first time and the roller, a heavy machine invariably towed by a single horse, is the best implement to try him on.

For a change, he's wearing blinkers. Horses' eyes allow them to see backwards and forwards without turning their heads very far in either direction, and badly broken animals almost invariably have to wear blinkers to stop them catching sight of the machine they're pulling. At the time when heavy horses were numerous, blinkers were made by saddlers to a range of different designs, each peculiar to their local area. There were shell-shaped blinkers and square ones. Scottish blinkers were half-moon shaped. As a general rule John uses plain bridles with chain harness and blinkers in the shafts. And almost without exception, he makes sure that a young horse about to be introduced to shafts in the field for the first time is wearing blinkers. It's playing safe, just as John wouldn't normally make a young horse have its debut in shafts on a warm summer's day – because of the flies and clegs (horse flies) buzzing around, poised to bite.

Once again, Sandy's had a hard day's work. The intention has been to tire him and it's worked. He stands motionless as the cart harness is put on his back. Then comes the moment of truth. David, holding one rein, brings him round to the front of the machine and quietly orders him to back into it. John, holding the other rein, stands at his head. As he steps gingerly backwards Sandy trips on the shafts. There's a brief moment of alarm as he jumps and stumbles forward. David strokes his nose and talks gently to him. Then he tries again to back the horse. As he does so John lifts the shafts and quickly fastens his side to the harness. Sandy doesn't move. He's content – and David and John are relieved.

'Normally you'd want three men restraining the horse for this job, one on either side of the head and one holding the reins. If they panic they'll start rearing and bucking. But because he's been such a quiet-natured horse we felt we'd probably be all right with just the two of us. And that was the case – almost! Yes, he did give a little hop. He's such a long-legged horse he more or less tripped over the shafts. Some horses would have sprung forward at that point. But he was fine.'

For almost an hour the three walk up and down the field, Sandy pulling the roller and getting used to shafts for the first time in his life, David striding behind with the reins and John at his head. 'We take all the precautions we possibly can,' John says. 'You can't be too careful with big horses like this. You rely on them doing what they're told to do.'

He remembers a Clydesdale he broke in 30 years ago. Winston. Not named with Churchill in mind, apparently, but just as stubborn nevertheless. 'I had three good men with me when I put him in the shafts,' John said. 'He had been a bit unpredictable. We had him pulling a roller up and down a field which was strewn with rough bits of manure, and it seemed as though he was relaxing. Then all of a sudden he started bucking. What had happened was that one of the men with me, a horse breaker called Jack Huddleston, had deliberately thrown a bit of manure on Winston's back and it upset him. We got the horse calmed down and he never bolted again. Jack said it was better that he got the temper out of him when he was first in the shafts than later on when he was working on the farm. And he was right. Winston turned out to be a great worker.

'Horse breakers would often break in horses in a month, but we prefer to take more time. Sometimes we'll take six months from start to finish. Maybe longer. We have such a lot of other things to do on the farm, we can't be dropping everything to do horse breaking every day. It's got to fit in with all the other work. Mind, Sandy's not the finished article yet. Breaking him in is just the first job. He's what we call a "green" horse. The next two years he has to be schooled. He'll be five years old before he's what we call a "made" horse – fit for any task and ready to work in anyone's hands.'

How much has it all cost? John reckons that if he adds up the purchase price of a foal, the expense of keeping it, vet's bills and the fee he would pay a horse breaker if he wasn't doing it himself, he'd have spent £1,200 to get a horse to the stage Sandy has just reached. Not as cheap as many might imagine, but a good investment nonetheless.

Drystone Walling

Drystone walls are an integral part of the countryside's appearance in the North Pennines. Rightly is it called an Area of Outstanding Natural Beauty. When snow carpets the ground in winter, the walls define the shape of the landscape, forming black interstices against the even whiteness. And in the setting sun on summer evenings there's an equally pleasing sight, as the walls throw long, even shadows across the fields.

Drystone walls are undaunted by any physical obstacle. They contain no mortar or cement, and yet they seem able to climb the steepest slopes, plunge into the deepest ravines and cling to the most, awkward of contours. That they last is proof of the skills of drystone wallers of years gone by.

Sillywrea is not the largest of farms but

there's as much as five miles of walls encircling its fields. They were built at some time between 1750 and 1850, 100 years that saw vast areas of unenclosed moorland and pasture confined by new stone walls. They didn't just mark the perimeter of the farm or the field divisions, they also provided an important feature in windswept upland areas: shelter for sheep and cattle. Some seem to run deliberately north to south to counter the prevailing west winds.

'A wall's a great thing for protecting ewes and lambs,' John says. 'Compared to a wall, a wire net doesn't provide much shelter.'

Whether the walls at Sillywrea were built by John's great-grandfather isn't clear. He bought the farm in 1848, so it's probable that most of the walls were already erected. It's very likely, though, that the limestone came from a source either on the farm or close to it, because small country quarries were numerous in the 18th and 19th centuries.

John's grandfather clearly didn't feel the walls were up to his high standards. 'He had a fetish about straightening out the boundary walls and he had a man called Dickinson who was stonewalling here all the year round. Two shillings (10p) a day is what he was paid. Mind, he did a good job.'

A beech tree has crashed down in a gale and knocked a 15-foot breach in one of the walls of an outlying field at Sillywrea. It's a repair job that needs to be done soon if animals are to be stopped from escaping. Sheep have the irritating knack of spotting lush grass on the far side of a wall and finding a hole to get through.

'I wouldn't win any prizes at a stone-walling competition,' John says drily. 'But I can get a wall to stop up. I'd say it was one of my favourite jobs on the farm. Frost's the worst thing for a stone wall. It alters the shape of the ground and sends the stones tumbling. We try and mend them as soon as they're down. It fair annoys me when I see people carrying wire and gates to stop a gap. By the time they've carried them there and put them across the hole they could have had the wall half up again.

'And another thing about walls: in some places they're getting huge grants to put them back up. Well, they should never be down in the first place!'

Repairing a gap in a drystone wall is a time-consuming task but at least it has one advantage: most of the materials are there already. When men were building new stretches of wall years ago they would use some stone cleared from nearby fields, but the bulk of it would have to be hauled to the site. Here, John and his son-in-law will just re-use the old stone.

They set off up the field with a horse and cart. In the back are a few tools necessary for the job: a couple of spades, a saw and a hammer. En route, just in case they fall short, they collect a few stones from a heap on the edge of one of the fields. These are stones brought to the surface by ploughs over the years and picked by generations of Dodds to prevent them blunting the blades of grass-cutting machines.

'We don't always bring the cart,' John says. 'Often there's no need. But sometimes we need to bring half a load of stones to a gap because some of the stones have vanished altogether. Folks from the towns sometimes take them for their rockeries. They've even taken squares of sod off the pastures to patch up their lawns. Aye, it takes some believing. But it's true. Mind, if I caught them they would know all about it!'

David sets to and saws up the fallen tree. He piles some of the pieces on to the cart. Beech is good firewood. It doesn't burn too quickly and gives off a good heat. It's worth salvaging.

John begins to clear the area at the foot of the wall. He can tell which stones were on the outside of the old wall. They're weathered and lichen-encrusted after being battered by the elements for two centuries. Others are dusty but unmarked by the passage of time. They must have been hidden on the inside of the wall. John's looking for the coping stones which fit along the top of the wall and the 'throughs' – large, flat stones which run the width of it. These valuable pieces are placed to one side.

Some stonewallers work with a wooden A-shaped template called a walling frame. It should mirror the dimensions of the section of a finished wall. The frame is propped up along the line of work, with strings running from it along either side of the wall to guide the builder.

The height and width of stone walls vary from area to area depending on the supply of stone. Walls are traditionally broad in the bottom and taper towards the top.

Like a house, a stone wall needs a firm foundation or the rain and frost will send it cascading down. David sets to work with the spade, digging out a shallow trench which is slightly wider than the wall and extends the length of the gap. Flat stones of an even thickness are laid along the trench and firmed into place with soil and rubble to form a level base. Then the building begins. Effectively what John and David are going to do is put up two wall faces with 'middling' (rubble) in the middle, the whole structure tied together by long through stones (known as 'thruffs' or 'thrufts' in Northumberland). As in bricklaying, bonding strength comes from laying one stone over the gap between two in the course below. This is called 'splitting (or crossing) the joints'.

As the wall rises, each layer of stone is set slightly further in so that a wall which may be three feet wide at the bottom narrows to only 18 inches at the top. The strings running from the walling frame provide the builder with a visual guide to the height, direction and batter (slope) of the wall.

What are the skills of a stone-waller? An eye for a stone and the place to put it, for one thing. It's said a good waller never handles a stone twice. He'll invariably slot it in somewhere the first time he picks it up, because experience will tell him there's always a place for a stone in a wall and where to find it. He'll use a mason's hammer sparingly, because time spent breaking a stone is time lost placing it.

David and John have reached the stage where the wall needs crowning. The pattern of coping stones varies from area to area. In some parts of the north of England, dry-stone wallers cut turf sods and lay them along the top of the wall in a style which is similar to the thick stone 'hedges' of the West Country. In parts of Cumbria the walls are topped with crenellations, but the style in Northumberland is more mundane. Coping stones are flat with a level edge. They're jammed on end, like a continuous stone 'crest' holding the top of the wall together.

It's taken John and David a few afternoons to remove the tree, clear the heap of stones and rebuild the gap. Full-time drystone wallers reckon they can work faster than that: they can rebuild five yards a day, provided the stone is in reasonable condition.

Stonewalling today is, not surprisingly, a lot more expensive than it was 100 years ago, when labour was cheap. Records show that at the end of the 19th century wallers were charging 6s 6d (about 32 pence) for a rood (seven yards). That's four pence a yard. Today these country craftsmen charge about £15 a yard. It may seem a gigantic increase, but no one would deny that they earn every penny of it.

Summer

Preparing the Land

It's the beginning of July. White clouds billow over the Roman Wall where it tops the Whin Sill three miles north of Sillywrea. Shorn sheep stand out like daisies on a green field to the west. In the hedgerows, wild roses are in bloom. David walks Dick and Davey sedately down a lane between two stone walls. They go through a gate into Lanefoot Field where two other men and three horses are already at work.

In a short while, anyone who might happen to be watching from the nearby road will be able to feast their eyes on a scene so rare they will have to pinch themselves: five horses in work harness pulling the sort of machines that vanished from the British countryside half a century ago. And doing it as part of their ordinary life – not for an agricultural show display or as a nostalgic reconstruction of the way things used to be.

These horses are sweating in the sun, eager for their lunchtime drink and feed. Their harness is not polished. It's well-worn and patched in places with string. The machines are dusty from work and the men who trudge behind them are silent because they have walked many miles this morning. They too are thinking about their dinners.

This particular field was ploughed by David in March and April and left to receive the full blast of the elements over the following months. It was going to be planted with turnips and mangolds. At least that was the plan. But three weeks of continuous rain in June – an unprecedented spell of poor weather, even for the north Pennines – have left the ground too heavy to be used as a seedbed. 'It's just like porridge,' John complains. 'We had to plough it all again.' The field is littered with large lumps of soil. It needs to be stirred and stirred – just like lumpy porridge – until it's ready. David has a couple of implements at his disposal for doing just that. And both, in common with all his machines, have a long history.

There is evidence of horse-drawn harrows being used to cultivate the earth and cover newly-sown seed as long ago as the Roman period. Harrows are featured on the Bayeux tapestry of 1080, and many documents from medieval times have illustrations of them. The early versions were no more than heavy lumps of wood with iron spikes fixed to the underside. And this is still the kind of thing David is using (although his hasn't got spikes). Towed by two horses in chain harness, the implement resembles a broad, flat sledge. In other parts of the country these machines were known as plank drags, rubbers or clot (clod) crushers. Here in the north-east it's called a scrubber. 'In prehistoric times they would have used branches or a tree trunk for this kind of work,' says David. 'I know it looks crude, but this particular machine is very effective for breaking the lumps down.'

The scrubber consists of six thick planks set at an angle into two beams. Made of oak, it's a heavy piece of equipment, and it's given extra weight either by having stones piled onto it or by the driver standing on it as the horses drag it across the land. As it travels over the surface it grinds down the balls of soil and creates a fine tilth.

It was specially made for John and David by a joiner at Jackson's sawmill in nearby Hexham. 'It was modelled on an old one we had, which was worn out. I took it down to Jackson's workshop and they made a new one, slightly bigger and heavier than the old one.' John says, 'You won't see many around these days. On farms where there are tractors they've got much bigger machines for breaking down the soil. But it's fine for horse work. We get a lot of use out of it.'

Part of the field still needs cultivating to a deeper depth. David looses out Dick and Davey from the scrubber and, clicking his tongue, makes them amble to the side of the field where a set of spring-tooth harrows are lying. He attaches the chains to the front of the harrows, and horses and harrows set off across the field. This kind of machine came into use in the 1890s. Some had seats to ride on but David has to walk behind his. Its 16 curved metal teeth (prongs) are flexible. There's a certain amount of give in them, so it's easier to drag than a rigid harrow. Similar (but much larger) harrows are hauled by tractors today.

John bought his set of spring-tooth harrows at a farm sale in the 1960s. He has a high opinion of these particular culti-vators: 'They're a grand thing for young horses because when they're just starting you can set the teeth very shallow, which means they're only light to pull, and as the horses get stronger and more experienced you can adjust the setting. But you have to be careful with them. The old horsemen used to say spring-tooth harrows were horse-killers because some farmers insisted the teeth should be set deep and they were murder for a horse to pull.'

Elsewhere in the field Norman Barber is working with a horse-drawn machine that perfectly fits the description of another of John's bargains'. It's a fertiliser drill, also known as a 'manure barrow'. John remembers where he bought it. 'We were at a sale at Silloth in Cumbria,' he recalls. 'A farm where there was a lot of horse-drawn machinery. The farmer must have been a bit of a collector in his own right. He'd gathered quite a lot of stuff together but he hadn't been using it on the land, so it was in good order.'

And the price? Deadpan, John says: '£11.' He seems to think he might have paid too much. Whatever the cost, the drill has been a faithful servant. Although it must be at least 60 years old, it still works well.

Granular fertiliser (referred to as 'artificial' by many farmers of John's generation) came into use on farms in the early 20th century as chemical companies developed compounds that boosted crops' growth rates and yields.

At Sillywrea, John and David use nitrogen-based fertiliser sparingly, but they

167

don't classify themselves as organic, or fertiliser-free. 'I don't believe in forced farming – pushing crops too much – but I have nothing against giving them a good start,' John says. 'We're up against it as it is, with the poor weather we get, the heavy clay we work with and the height we are above sea level, so anything which assists our crops we welcome.'

The fertiliser drill, pulled by a single horse in shafts, is one of the larger machines on the farm. About 10 feet wide, it's basically a big coffin-like box supported by two large iron wheels. Like many implements from the era of horses, it's driven by these land wheels. Fertiliser poured from bags into the container on the top flows through gaps onto a row of seven saucers at the back of the spreader. A series of cogs connect the axle to a rotating bar fitted with metal fingers. As they go round, the fingers flick the fertiliser granules off the saucers and onto the ground.

The flow of the granules from the hopper can be adjusted by widening the gap at the base of the box. Crops like turnips receive a heavier dressing of fertiliser at Sillywrea.

How do you know you're not spreading the same area twice? Horsemen say that so long as you follow the wheelmarks from the previous pass, you should be fine. But to make doubly certain, the machine can be knocked out of gear at the headland by pulling a lever. That way you don't waste fertiliser as you're turning to begin a new row. 'Oh, they're a grand machine,' John says. 'We've got another one which we use for powdered fertiliser. Obviously with some crops you don't need to apply so much and you don't have to stop so often to fill up. Depending on how thinly you're putting it on you can cover a lot of ground quite quickly.'

Three times the land has been crumbled by the scrubber and combed by the spring tooth harrows. It finally has the right consistency for the next job: raising drills for turnips.

These brassicas, which thrive in cold, damp climates, were a staple part of the diet of Europe's poor for centuries before potatoes arrived from South America.

They owe their place in British agriculture to Viscount Townshend (1674–1738), a diplomat who, on his retirement in 1730, turned enthusiastically to running his country estate at Raynham in Norfolk. As every student of history knows, Charles 'Turnip' Townshend is credited with transforming the humble turnip from a garden vegetable into a farm crop grown on a vast scale. This revolutionised livestock production. Until that time most people killed their livestock around Martinmas (11 November) because it was too expensive to store the amount of hay needed to feed them on all winter. This left too much meat coming onto the market at once. People dried some of their beef and lamb in peat smoke or pickled the meat in brine but these preserving methods were not always successful. Townshend changed all that. He imported the seed of hardy turnips from Holland and showed that farmers who grew them on a field scale could at last keep cattle and sheep through the winter by feeding them generous helpings of these nutritious roots.

In farming these days turnips are less popular than they used to be but John and David, who still grow several acres, swear by them. 'We're going to sow some soft turnips for the sheep. It's possibly a bit late in the summer but we'll get a good crop. If you put them in too soon they can get mildew and go rotten. They make ideal fodder for sheep in the winter.'

To ensure a good crop of turnips John likes to grow them on ridges. This entails 'raising drills', taking a drill plough with two mouldboards and 'stitching' the field from one end to the other. The plough John is using has two wheels at the front which help to take the weight off the arms and shoulders of the driver, but many double-mouldboard ploughs didn't have wheels and they were considered to be hard work by ploughmen. In fact, the use of wheels on this type of plough was almost a geographical feature. East of Sillywrea, most had wheels, but west of the farm they didn't. There was often no clear reason for these regional preferences, but they persisted throughout the country in the days before the mass production of equipment.

A good piece of raised drilling is a master-piece, the even ridges dark and light across the field. John insists that it is a real art – and one that has almost disappeared for good.

John says, 'You can either drill straight, or you can't. I've always been able to keep a straight line. Take my advice: never look back. Always look ahead between the horses' heads. The drill plough has a marker but don't follow the mark all the time. Use it as a guide. Sometimes you have to be to one side of the mark and sometimes to the other. Oh, it's a grand job, raising drills. It's especially nice if the land's worked right. It's one of my favourite jobs of the whole year.

'The great thing is to have two good drilling horses. If you have one that's pulling away in front of the other one, or wobbling about, it doesn't help. They say it's a poor man who blames his tools, but having a bad horse doesn't help.'

In former times, farm workers were criticised if there was even the smallest of kinks in their drills. They were supposed to be gun-barrel straight. 'There was a young chap at the mart one day and he was getting a lot of skit because of his drills, and to be truthful, they were dreadful. Very wobbly. And there was an old farmer standing nearby listening, and he said to the lad: "Pay no heed to them. You'll have more turnips at the backend of the year. You're bound to: your drills are far longer!"'

Following John along the drills he's just raised is Norman, with a single horse in the shafts of a turnip drill. It's a Sellar drill, the name of the manufacturer (Sellars were based at Huntly in Aberdeenshire) in bold relief on the cast-iron lid of the seedbox. Once, there were thousands of these drills at work on farms in the north of England and Scotland.

172

The machine runs on two concave rollers which look like ship's capstans. They smooth and firm the tops of the drills in front of a coulter (knife). The coulter cuts a gash in the soil, into which the seed falls. A spindle, linked to the rollers via a shaft and a series of cogs, turns a row of brushes and spoons inside the two small seedboxes, sending the seeds down the planting pipes. The hole at the bottom of the seedbox can be altered to take different sizes of seed.

This is a direct descendant of a drill invented in 1788 by the Reverend James Cooke of Heaton Morris near Manchester, whose prototype used similar small cups to collect the seed from the seedbox and deposit them down the planting tubes.

Norman pours some of the tiny black turnip seeds into the hopper and closes the lid, the clank of metal on metal a familiar noise to the men who used these machines back in the early years of this century. Shifting a gear across, he sets off with the seeds trickling down the two tubes and into the top of the ridges.

Bent low over the handles and controlling the horse through the reins in his hands, Norman is doing several things at once. He's making sure the horse walks in the bottom of the drill, he's trying to sow in a straight line and he's checking that the seed is flowing smoothly. 'What you're trying to avoid is a miss, where maybe a larger than usual seed blocks the hopper,' he says. 'If that keeps happening, there'll be fewer turnips for the sheep.'

And, just as important, someone might notice. There will be an obvious gap when all the plants are growing which will catch the eye of passers-by. It's a matter of pride to the horsemen that all the jobs are done right.

The Professor

Over the years a steady stream of luminaries have beaten a path to Sillywrea to see for themselves how the farm operates with just a few horses to do all the work. In the mid1980s the Ministry of Agriculture even appointed a farming adviser whose sole job was to encourage the use of horsepower (the equine kind) on farms. He made his way from his base in the Midlands to John's exposed farm in Northumberland and talked to John about his farming system.

'Nice chap,' John recalls. 'But I don't think it came to anything. I told him I couldn't see horses making a come-back on a large scale.'

The latest boffin to drop in at Sillywrea is Professor David Harvey, Head of Agricultural Economics at Newcastle University. The pipe-puffing Professor at least has the right background to understand what John and David are up to: he was brought up on a tenanted farm on the top of the Marlborough Downs in Wiltshire. But while David Harvey recognises some of the facets of Sillywrea from his own childhood, he's having his eyes opened too. Working their way laboriously across a grass field are John, David, Norman and Richard.

They are picking stones.

It's a scene which vanished from most parts of rural Britain more than a century ago. Farm workers' wives and children were paid a pittance to pick basketfuls of stones from ploughed fields and dump them on the roads around a village. The Sillywrea gang have made one concession to the 21st century: they're using plastic buckets to collect the stones before tipping them into a horse-drawn cart. David Wise has a graipe (fork) to dig out the more deeply-embedded ones. Successive cultivations have brought the stones to the surface, and unless they're removed they'll severely damage the blades of the grass-cutting machines which are due to start work in this field in a month's time.

David Harvey chats to John to the accompaniment of a steady stream of dull thuds as stones hit the wooden base of the cart. John tells him about the beef and sheep farming system at Sillywrea. He explains that he doesn't breed Clydesdales or show them. He just likes to work them. 'We're content the way we are,' he says. 'They're both work and pleasure.'

Back at the farm; the Professor gives his reaction to his visit. 'Working a farm like this with just horses and the occasional contractor, that is extremely unusual,' he admits. 'But how unusual it will be in the future is a bit hard to predict. I mean, it's a glorious part of the world, isn't it? Plenty of people would give their right arm to live here. But most of us have rather different aspirations for what we want to do with our lives. We want to drive new cars and have new televisions and all the new gadgets that go in our houses. We want to take holidays from time to time.

'There aren't too many people around who relish their work and their life as much as John does. He and David obviously get a lot of enjoyment out of farming the way they do, otherwise they wouldn't keep on doing it. They don't have a massive investment in machinery because they're picking it up at relatively cheap prices at farm sales. And their labour is their own. It's damned hard work, but as long as you enjoy the work, and they obviously do, you can still make a living.

'They must be worried how much longer they'll be able to keep doing it if farming continues to be in its current depression. But farming can't stay in the doldrums indefinitely. There may be a thinning out of farms but sooner or later prices will pick up and things will get better.'

Grass Cutting

On another part of the farm a field lying next to a neighbour's has been prepared for seeds. Coincidentally, so has the neighbour's – and both farms are going to sow grass. The difference is that the neighbour's crop is put in by a 100-horsepower tractor and a power-driven drill, whereas John's using a drill that's almost an antique and one-horsepower! However, he's generous in his praise of the neighbour's handywork: 'He's made a grand job of it,' he says. But he's also conscious that his neighbour might be leaning over the fence to have a look at his crop of grass, just as someone in a suburban estate might watch how his neighbour's newly seeded lawn is coming on. 'Of course you're interested in what's going on all around you,' John smiles. 'It wouldn't be natural if you weren't.

'This field has been ploughed for years and years and it's time it had a change. So we're sowing it down to grass.

'It's quite a tricky job sowing the grass seeds and getting them to come even and level.'

Just as grass crops have improved, so have the sounds of haytime changed over the last 200 years. Walk through rural Britain in high summer in the early 19th century and all you would hear would be the swish of the scythe as labourers steadily cut their way through fields of grass. Then, as mechanisation gradually came into farming, the chatter of knives in horsedrawn reapers took over. Now, in the 21st century, grass-cutting has entered an industrial age and the coun-tryside from May onwards is dominated by the drone of tractor-mounted drum mowers.

There's still a place at Sillywrea for the scythe, one of the countryman's most valued friends. John uses it to cut bracken, which is a useful thatching material to insulate a heap of turnips from frosts.

The origin of this crop-cutting tool isn't known but it certainly goes back as far as the Roman era. Early manuscripts show scythe handles as being straight, which would have made them hard to use, but in more modern times makers of scythes (usually village blacksmiths) have curved the handle to give it better balance and make it more efficient.

Cutting grass with a scythe was harder work than cutting corn. The best mowers went at it steadily, keeping a constant pace but not rushing. If a man tackled a hayfield with a scythe and cut an acre of grass in a day he was doing well.

Farm workers often went out to mow at dawn, when the dew was still on the grass and it cut better. Scythes would soon lose their sharpness, and many people considered that sharpening a scythe was as great a skill as wielding it. Before the advent of the manufactured sharpening stone such as the carborundum, workers carried their own wooden 'strickles' whose pitted

179

wooden surface would be sprinkled with mutton fat (carried in a horn) and soft sand (kept in a drawstring bag). Laid flat against the blade and properly stroked in a curving motion, these abrasive whetstones quickly sharpened a scythe dulled by hard work. Wrongly used, they would cause the scythe to lose its edge, and it would have to be taken back to the farm to be sharpened on a grindstone. 'By Jove,' says John, 'if you can't sharpen a scythe you'll not cut much.'

Labourers in the past often cut grass in gangs, working at three-yard intervals to allow room to swing the blade. It was easy to see where there had been poor work because there were tufts of half-cut grass across the field. The 1900 copy of the farmers' bible, Fream's *Elements of Agriculture*, states gravely: 'It is very annoying for a good scythesman to have to follow a bad one.' The technique was simple, the book said: 'When mowing, a man should place his legs wide apart so as to bring his back into the best position for it to exercise its strength, for mowing should be done by means of a body stroke rather than by the arms. The arms should act chiefly as guiding or connecting rods between the man and the scythe, in the same way as a skilful oarsman exerts his powers from the back and by the use of his legs, instead of pulling the stroke through with his arms.

> Rain in May
> Makes good hay

In the days before the introduction of the now-ubiquitous polythene bags for storing big bales of fresh-cut grass as silage, hay was the fodder all farmers made to feed to their animals through the winter. Farmers always talked in reverential tones of 'June Hay'. It was like a fine wine or a valuable gemstone. Rarely achieved, but very special when it was. Hay won in June is not only tastier to livestock but also more digestible and nourishing than hay made later in the summer. But not everyone can make it. In the upland areas of Northumberland, the grass grows more slowly than it does in the valleys. It's not usually ready to cut until July.

For a small farm, Sillywrea grows a lot of grass for hay. A quarter of its 200 acres is cut each year, a sizeable task for horse-drawn machines. Once David and John start cutting, the aim is to have fields of hay in different stages of readiness: some just cut, some drying, some turned once or twice, and some ready to be led into the barn. An anxious eye is kept on the forecast. If the weather is unpredictable ('catchy' they call it in the north because it's a question of catching the hay while you can), farmers don't want to have too much grass cut, because as it lies in the swathe it loses its quality. 'It's an obvious thing to say, but you can only make hay when the sun's shining,' says David. 'So it can be a pleasure or a frustration, depending on what sort of weather you're having. It can be infuriating to have a field of hay almost ready and then to have it moistened by a shower of rain. But we always get it in the end.' And, most important, they generally get some good quality hay for the horses.

Just as men with scythes were despatched to the field for an early start, so David and John like to get up early to start cutting grass – at 4.30 in the morning. The sooner they get going, the more they can cut. It's cooler for the horses in the early part of the day, and there are fewer 'clegs' (horse flies) and midges around to annoy them. That's particularly important when working a young, fidgety horse which is bothered by flies in the heat of the day.

'If you start at daybreak you can knock a

lot of grass down by ten o'clock,' says John. 'And if it's good winning (drying) weather, you're getting ahead.'

The mower's been checked over and greased, the horses have been fed and David's in the toolshop with one of the reaper knives locked in the vice. He's involved in a last-minute bout of blade sharpening. 'Mower knives need to be sharpened regularly,' he explains. 'If not, they can break and then it's a long delay.' The cutter bar, usually measuring about four and a half feet, is subjected to a great deal of wear and tear in a field of grass, especially if the crop has aged. Having a spare knife (wrapped in two protective pieces of board to prevent injury) is essential.

The horse mowers used by John and David are drawn by two horses harnessed either side of a long draught pole. The driver rides on the machine on a sprung seat, from which he controls the horses through the reins and adjusts the height of the mower with a lever. A foot pedal puts the machine in and out of gear. The machine is carried on two large iron travelling wheels which are slatted for a better grip. These wheels drive the cutting blade via a hub gearbox and connecting rod. Most cutter bars in Britain were mounted to the right of the driving wheels so that the field could be cut in a clockwise direction.

But in the village of Newton, near Corbridge, about a dozen miles from Sillywrea, there was a small agricultural firm called Simms which specialised in manufacturing reapers with cutter bars on the left. The firm closed years ago but their reapers are fondly remembered by those who used them as strong, heavy machines with high gearing, so that even when the horses were picking their way slowly through a heavy crop of grass the knife was still running fast enough to cut it.

When a new field of grass was about to be mown for hay, a small square was cut by hand at the gate so that the horses would not trample it flat as the reaper was being made ready for cutting. The first two passes with the mower were made the 'wrong' way round the field, leaving up to a foot of grass close to the field wall or hedge. Even though it was often full of weeds, this thin strip was 'hacked out' by scythe to leave nothing at all standing. Neatness was everything. At Sillywrea, John used to do this until the 1960s. 'Myself and our neighbour Bob Davidson would be the last farmers in this district to hack out the dyke backs round the hayfields. But in the end we even stopped doing that. There wasn't enough time.'

These days they cut the first swathe with the mower about 10 feet in from the edge and then turn round and cut the next swathe closer to the 'dyke' (hedge or wall). Some of the standing grass is trodden underfoot by the horses' hooves. The taskmaster farmers of old wouldn't approve, but David has to be practical. He's working, as usual, with Davey and Dick, who are yoked either side of the mower's pole. He has to make sure that the pole is at the right height – at its head it must be a yard from the ground to ensure easy draught and correct cutting.

After dinner, John joins David in the hayfield and it makes a wondrous sight as they cut one after the other, two pairs of horses pulling mowing machines from the 1940s. Both are Albions, which were made by Harrison, McGregor and Co. of Leigh in Manchester. John has four Albions and he can remember exactly where he bought each of them: two from a farm sale at Lazonby in Cumbria, one from a sale at Silloth, and one from the nearby village of Catton. Albions were regarded as among the most reliable of horse mowing machines, and while these have lasted far longer than anyone would have imagined, John has found that they also have their flaws. 'The weak point on an Albion is the casing where the connecting rod joins the knife head. That often breaks. The sections of the knives wear out too but we've got a good collection of knives which we've bought at sales over the years. We don't miss a chance to buy up old mower knives if we can, because one day there won't be any left.'

A newly planted field of grass will present more problems than an old meadow, because the grass is thicker. The mower will frequently clog up and the horses have to be stopped and backed up so that the cut grass can be cleared from the cutter bar. Rather than cut round a block of grass, the horse men will cut one way only and then raise the bar, put it out of gear and walk back to cut the same way again. The same happens if it's very windy or has been unduly wet, and the grass is lying flat.

In a wet summer, making hay can be a testing experience. John can recall hay that he's harvested in really bad years turning almost black in the fields. 'Like dust from a coal mine, that's what it was,' he recalls. 'But then other years you have an easier time. You just have to be patient. If it's raining there's not a lot you can do about it.'

How quickly can a pair of horses cut grass with a mower? John answers with pride. 'You can knock it down at a fair old rate if the conditions are right,' he says. 'I know the tractor men might laugh at what we do, but when we have to work fast, we can. I reckon two teams of horses can cut three-quarters of an acre an hour if there are no hold-ups.'

A Summer Sale

Bygones. The word leaps out of the advert in the local paper, catching David's eye. It's a Friday lunchtime and David's indulging himself in one of his weekly pleasures: scanning the farming pages of the *Hexham Courant*. He reads out a passage to John.

Large and interesting collection of vintage tractors and cars. Field of horse-drawn machinery. Sundry household items. Bygones.

It's an advertisement for an auction sale to be held by Hexham and Northern Marts 30 miles away at Healey Mill Farm, in the village of Netherwitton near Morpeth in Northumberland. The old man who ran the farm has died and everything he assembled in a lifetime on the land will have to come under the auctioneer's hammer. John and David decide to go. It's mid-July and they should carry on haymaking, but the prospect of picking up some horse-drawn equipment – hopefully at knockdown prices – is too good to miss. With the disappearance of heavy horses from the British countryside, the machines which once were hauled by those magnificent animals have also gone for good. At least, most of them have. That's why it's increasingly important for David and John to go to sales.

David says: 'A lot of the implements we use are 60 to 70 years old. You can't go out to the agricultural machinery dealers and buy a new one. You've got to go to farm sales and hope to pick them up there. Occasionally we hear of a broken-down implement standing behind an old wall on a farm somewhere and we'll go and have a look at it, and perhaps we'll buy it if we think we can fix it. But horse implements are getting harder and harder to find. Sales are the main place.'

The word 'bygones' in the advert is what's sparked their interest. John knows that boxes of jumble buried in dusty corners of barns might contain something of use to him. His encyclopaedic knowledge of horse tack and parts for horsedrawn implements means he can spot a bargain. There's a drawback, however. The mention of bygones sends a signal to a different group – the people who deal in antiques and collectables. They may compete with the horsemen for something which is 'quaint', although of no practical value to them, and this will inflate the bidding. 'At one time we used to pay little more than scrap price for bits and pieces we bought at farm sales, but that's all changed now,' John says. 'Antique dealers and collectors have seen to that. I could pick up a horse-drawn implement in good condition for £15, 20 or 30 years ago, but those days have passed. Now you're more likely to pay £50.'

It may not sound much by most people's standards. Certainly, compared to modern tractor equipment costing thousands of pounds, such sums are minute. But John's a canny northern farmer. His farming system has only survived because over the years he's managed to buy horse-drawn machinery without paying very much for it.

David is a chip off the old block when it comes to sales. 'Often there'll be a heap of scrap at a sale – loads of old bits and pieces lumped together in one lot – and we'll go and have a sniff round to see what we can find. We're on the lookout for anything that may be of use to us: spare parts, plough wheels, tines for hay turners. A lot of people won't recognise these objects because they're not working with them every day A single plough sock will be chucked on the scrap heap because they don't believe anyone will want it. But it could plough us 30 acres. With any luck, the auctioneer will think these bits of scrap aren't valuable. But they have a value to us and we try and get them for as low a price as possible.

'Our main job, though, is to buy horse-drawn implements. It's reached the stage where if we find something of real use to us, be it a plough, a turner or a hay rake, we try and buy it. We may have a similar machine at home, but the supply overall is drying up. They're not making these things any more, and they're getting harder and harder to find at sales. So you bid for them whenever you have the chance.'

The men set off across Northumberland, their journey taking them past many familiar sights. A sea of white cotton grass covers the ground surrounding one of the landmarks of the district, the 100 foot Stublick Chimney, built in 1859 to suck off poisonous fumes from the Langley Smelt Mills which produced lead in the 100 years up to 1887. The chimney stands as a local memorial to the workers who gave their lives to the lead industry of the 18th century.

The road leads past castles and ruined towers. Perhaps it's not surprising that Northumberland is the least populated of England's counties. For centuries it was a highly dangerous place to live in, as Scots and English fought to control it.

John and David arrive at the sale as the sun bursts through the clouds. It's almost ten o'clock. The first lot comes up for auction at 11, so they've only given themselves an hour to poke about the thousands of items on offer. The location is idyllic. This was once a working mill which also had land for growing crops and raising animals. Over the years, milling declined and farming took over. But the approach to the place carries a reminder of its past. A rutted track winds down through fields full of cow parsley and buttercups and crosses a shallow ford over the River Wansbeck before reaching the small group of 19th-century stone buildings that make up the farm.

Laid out on the grass beside the mill is a collection of artefacts which would not look out of place in a museum of rural life. There are hay knives – V-shaped spades with sharpened blades which carved huge wedges out of a hay 'mow'. The broad handles are pockmarked with woodworm and worn with use, but they're a reminder of an era when hay was stacked loose, and balers and black plastic bags hadn't been dreamed of. There are sickles and scythes, relics of pre-combine harvester days when a field of corn had to be 'opened up', the first swathe cut by scythe to allow horses pulling reapers to make a clean start. There are draining spades, muck forks, byre shovels, mells (post hammers), pickaxes, sledge hammers. There are slashers and bill-hooks for hedge-laying, and grindstones, which were used to sharpen everything from sheep shears to the farmer's own pocket knife. There are boxes of joiners' tools, tins of nails, rasps, awls, hacksaws, augers, battered milk churns, blunt kitchen utensils, iron pots, chipped enamel bread bins, tyres, small engines, rusty pre-war bicycles, bootmakers' lasts, sack-weighing scales, beehives and ropes.

Above: Starting young: John Dodd, aged nine, with his two Shetland ponies, Jessie (left) and Mousey.
Below: John's father, George's Clydesdale mare Jewell took first prize at the Haltwhistle Show in 1922 and went on to breed a string of winners.

Above: Haytime at Sillywrea in 1928, with a mare
called Dinah in the shafts of a hayrake. The same haymaking machines are used today.
Below: Photographed in 1903, John's father George at
the age of four with his parents, George and Sarah,
and his sister Annie.

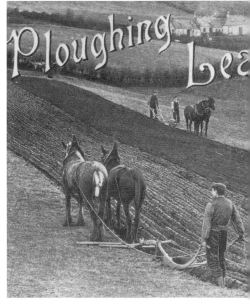

Above: Threshing day in the early 1900s. It took at least a dozen men to make the job go smoothly.
Below left: 'If you can't sharpen your scythe, you won't cut grass.'
Below right: Ploughing lea, 'the pleasantest disguise manual labour can take'.

Above: Handling hay was hard work: men building a
stack with hay at the turn of the century.

Above: Drying the swathe on a nineteenth century farm.
Below: John turning hay. Despite being over a hundred years apart, these two pictures show a remarkably similar scene.

Above: Cutting grass with a single-horse mower in the 1890s. The men following the mower are tidying up the swathes of grass with their wooden hayrake.
Below: Taking a break. John's family (his mother Mary, then still single, is second left in the white hat) enjoying a picnic in the hayfield in the mid-1920s.

Above: A horse-drawn reaper at work in the cornfield at the end of the 19th century, when sheaves were still tied by hand.
Below: Sides shaved and roofs thatched, an imposing group of stacks on a farm in Northumberland in 1905.

Above left: 'The best haytime in living memory', John yoking a hay turner in the hot summer of 1976.
Above right: Son of the soil. John's life-long friend, ploughman Tom Forster.
Below: John and Tom Forster ploughing stubble in the Kiln Field at Sillywrea.

Above: Keeping a straight furrow, John ploughing with a perfectly matched pair of horses.
Below: Steady work for horse and cart: the daily job of leading muck.

Above: Preparing the land for sowing corn. David Wise harrowing a field.
Below: Norman Barber's horses pulling a scrubber to break up the clods of earth.

Above: Spring at Sillywrea. While David works in the background, Cheviot ewes and lambs enjoy a warm April day. *Below:* Two faithful friends. John with Sandy (left) and Robin.

Above left: Maggie Dodd
Above right: Frances Wise with her sheepdogs Jan (left)
and Fly.
Above centre left: David with Davey, his favourite horse.
Below: Straight as a gun barrel: John raising turnip drills.

Above left: They may be known as 'gentle giants', but David says a lot of experience is needed to handle Clydesdales correctly.

Above right: Richard Wise with his Shetland pony, Penny.

Below: John with the grass seed drill, bought in 1939 and still going strong.

Above left: Rolling the grass. One of the important jobs in spring.
Above and below: Haytime at Sillywrea, 2000. Fewer people working on the land than a century ago, but similar equipment still being used.

Above left: 'The quietest horse we've ever had.' John with Sandy. *Above right:* Decked out in show harness, Sandy and Davey at an exhibition of horse-drawn ploughing in Northumberland, 2000. *Below:* Sandy gives John, David and Richard a ride home on the bogey.

Above: A scene which hasn't changed for 150 years. Muck heaps deposited five yards apart, to be spread in spring before the grass starts to grow again.
Below: Homeward bound: bringing the horses in after a long day in the fields drilling another year's corn.

On a bench in a murky outhouse lies another link with the past, a seed fiddle. Introduced to Britain from the USA at the end of the 19th century by a Liverpool firm, J.H. Newton, this device revolutionised broadcast sowing of seed, which hitherto had been done by hand. Suspended on straps in front of the sower like a cinema usherette's ice-cream tray, it held a shallow sack from which seed fell through a narrow gate onto a disc. A rod attached to the disc by a leather thong was worked to and fro, like a bow sawed by a violinist, spinning the seed from the disc in regular arcs onto the soil. It was reckoned a man with a fiddle could sow up to four acres an hour.

Clustered in the overgrown farmyard are other mementoes of an earlier age: a butter churn, a mangle, stone drinking troughs, a wooden wheelbarrow, an old water pump, a sack hoist and a paraffin drum. Nearby stand a corn crusher for milling oats, a winnowing machine for separating chaff from grain and a turnip cutter, used to slice turnips and mangolds into small chunks. Many a retired farm worker will remember chilly winter mornings turning the machine's handle and chopping turnips, their characteristic sweet smell rising from the pile of chips as the swill (wire basket) filled up.

The farmer at Healey Mill was an avid hoarder of old motor vehicles, so it's not surprising that the sale has drawn a flock of vintage car enthusiasts. They're poring over treasures like a 1923 Sunbeam motorbike, parts for Model T Fords, handbooks for lorries including a 1902 Foden, and a Fowler steam engine catalogue. Members of the local tractor restoration club are gazing longingly at a Massey Ferguson 55K, bought at the Royal Show in 1947, and a dilapidated 1944 Oliver Row Crop 70. These two elderly tractors are the biggest attractions in the sale. They're lot numbers 455 and 456, the last of the day, a deliberate move on the part of the auctioneer. That way, people will stay to the end.

David and John make straight for a closely-cropped meadow where 40 implements – ancient and modern – are lined up. The catalogue lists a few horse-drawn items: three grasscutters, a hay tedder, a potato digger, two rakes, a plough, a seed drill and a cultivator. Excitement mounts as they cross the field to look at the machines, but their disappointment is palpable when they get up close to them. There's a Martin's cultivator dating from 1900, but it's so badly rusted it's past redemption. 'Scrap,' says John, 'that's all it's good for.' The Bamford hay rake is also clogged up with rust. John predicts someone will buy it for the wheels – there's a trend for incorporating them into gates for country houses. The shaft on the Ransome's potato digger is broken and the plough's slightly damaged. It's a sorry lot.

The sale has begun, and auctioneer Brian Rogerson strides into the field, a Pied Piper followed by a vast crowd of onlookers and potential buyers. He leads them from lot to lot, knocking each down with his quickfire chatter. There's a considerable amount of interest in the horse-drawn machines but it's not translated into high prices. The hayrake only makes £12 and one of the mowers just £50. Although incomplete, the plough sells for £100. Will it end up on the lawn in front of a pub? Or will it be restored by a collector? It's difficult to say.

The multitude surges into the farmyard to witness the next part of the sale. John and David are swept along by the throng. The auctioneer is working fast. Someone pays £2 for a watering can. The seed fiddle goes for £25. There seems to be a buyer for everything. People are going mad over the vintage car spares.

John's got his eye on a box full of new ropes. They start at £5 and go up in £2 bids to £18, where the other bidder drops out and they're knocked down to John. His face remains expressionless. He's got the bargain he came for, but he's not showing it. Three augers are next, their corkscrew shafts held aloft for all to see. John, from his brief apprenticeship as a joiner, knows the value of these carpenters' tools. But he's not going to pay over the odds, so he starts them at £1 and raises them in £1 bids before shaking his head at £9. He'd set a price in his mind and he wasn't going to go over it.

Carrying their purchases back to the pickup, John and David discuss the sale. 'You never know what you're going to find,' says John. 'The implements were disappointing. They were in such a poor state of repair. But on a farm like ours where there are horses, ropes are always useful. And I got some joiners' clamps for next to nothing. Best of all, I've seen a lot of people I know and had a good crack. You catch up on the gossip at a sale like this. It's been a good day out. And hopefully, there'll still be time to work in the hay when we get back to the farm.'

Model Makers

The camera's click makes an incongruous sound in the hayfield, a modern interruption to a timeless scene. The man taking pictures isn't looking for conventional images, however. Not for him the horse hauling a hayrake over the rim of the field against a backdrop of a cloudless Northumberland sky. Instead, Ray Ayres is photographing the details of haymaking with heavy horses. He's interested in the curve of the reins across a horse's flanks, the angle of a lever jutting out of a machine, the way a horseman bends to his task. He shoots off roll after roll of film in his desire to grasp how everything works. To complete his research, he carries a metal measuring tape and a notebook. The exact dimensions of everything he's photographed have to be written down.

Ray is master sculptor for Border Fine Arts, a firm which makes the painted figurines so avidly sought after by thousands of collectors. The range of models produced is huge. They include collections based on the books of James Herriot, A.A. Milne and Beatrix Potter. But wildlife, farming and countryside subjects are their speciality.

In 1990 Ray decided to design a few horse-farming figures. Delving into collections of old photographs, he'd built up a detailed picture of the models he'd like to sculpt. But something was missing: he needed to meet someone who kept cart horses so that he could capture the magic of these giant animals genuinely at work on a farm. It took some time. 'I found there are plenty of people who still have Clydesdales but in almost all cases they do it as a hobby. There was no one left using horses on a down to earth, day-to-day basis. Or that's how it seemed. Then someone said they thought there was a farmer in Northumberland who still used horses. We made some enquiries and that's how I came across John Dodd.'

The first model based on John was called 'Stout Hearts'. It features two Clydesdale horses ploughing lea (grass). In some ways, it's an idealised version of the real thing: the furrows are perfectly even, the traditional blue paint on the plough body is unmarked, the hames glisten silver and the horse collars are well polished. The farmer, in typical attire of cap, collarless shirt, waistcoat, corduroy trousers and leggings, is a lot tidier than he might actually be. But in other respects, the model is true to its original. The hands, wrapped round with reins, grasp the plough stilts in just the same way that John's do. The harness is exactly as it should be. And most impressive of all, the sculptor has captured the gait of the horses, one in the furrow bottom, the other on the land, both straining to draw the plough through the ground.

A second model, 'Supplementary Feeding', featured a farmer feeding mangolds to sheep from the back of a horse-drawn cart. The cart is unmistakably John's. It is the same colours of green and red and has the same worn boards. The cart harness is faithfully reproduced, and the reins (tiny filaments on a model this size) are tied to the cart top, just as they would be while the farmer unloads the fodder – here, to two Cheviot ewes and a lamb waiting for their breakfast. This model has an element of humour in it. The horse waiting quietly in the shafts has its head turned round to see where the succulent mangolds are landing, as if to say: 'How about me?' There's also a Border collie alertly watching the proceedings. One of the ewes (the one closest to the lamb) is eyeballing the dog. Its attitude seems to warn: keep away from my baby!

'I suppose we're striking a chord in people's memories,' Ray says. 'There's no getting away from it. There's a strong sense of nostalgia for the past, especially among people who have close links with the land. People like to remember how often they saw a certain country scene when they were younger. We're trying to recreate that moment in time for them.'

Nearly 10 years have passed since 'Stout Hearts' was issued. Ray has returned to Sillywrea to start work on a new project: five scenes of haymaking on horse farms. It will be a limited edition series: 950 copies of each model. Ray has done his research on the first model in the series – a pair of horses pulling a grass mower. The model is already taking shape back at his studio at the Border Fine Arts factory in Langholm, Dumfriesshire. Now, with the arrival of haytime, he can continue his preparations for the remaining four.

The second in the series is to be a single horse with a hay turner. Ray doesn't have to go far to find inspiration. Norman is at work in the next field, riding up and down the swathes of grass on a machine which flips them over, allowing the wind and sun to dry the underside. Before these machines were introduced in 1896 swathes were turned by hand, rows of labourers working with rakes to lift and aerate the drying hay. With mechanisation, two swathes could be turned at once by curved tines powered by a shaft connected to the turner's two land wheels. Over the years, John and David have collected seven hay turners of different designs: three Blackstones, three Massey-Harris and 'a Scotch one I can't remember the name of but we call it a Dickie turner'. As with other implements, it's important to have a machine to wheel out if there's a breakdown. The tines have a habit of snapping off hay turners, and although John carries a toolkit with him in the hayfield and it's a relatively quick repair job, it's sometimes better to get another turner and keep going, particularly in good weather.

The third haymaking implement in the Border Fine Arts series is a horse-drawn sweep, a crude American implement which appeared on British farms in the 1880s. Hay which had been turned two or three times until it was dry was gathered into windrows (wide swathes formed by joining two rows together). The sweep was a wooden beam with six wooden spikes projecting from it. Dragged by a single horse with trace chains and guided by barrow-like handles from behind, the sweep's points slid beneath the hay and steadily collected it. When it was full, the driver lifted the sweep by the handles so that the spikes dug in the ground. As the horse continued to walk forwards the sweep did a somersault, leaving the collected hay behind in a heap.

David and John have restored a hay sweep in the implement shed at Sillywrea. It's rarely used, but they've brought it out to show Ray how it works. As David discovers when he uses it for the first time in a hayfield, operating a sweep is hard work. Holding the reins as well as the two sweep handles is difficult in the extreme. Sweeps in the north were known as 'tumbling Toms' or 'tumbling Geordies' and in Scotland as 'tumbling Tams'. It was an appropriate name. Avoiding the heavy spikes as they went head over heels wasn't easy. And on uneven ground there was another hazard: the points of the sweep could become embedded in a ridge in the field and would frequently snap off.

In Scotland and the north of England, areas with a heavier rainfall than the south, it wasn't usually possible to cart all the hay into barns at once. In very wet summers, the hay was collected into lines of small heaps called 'kyles', which provided marginally better protection for the crop than leaving it to rot in rows. But kyles had to be shaken out and dried before the hay could be brought in, and this extra work prolonged the whole process. It was far easier when the weather was settled and the mounds of hay gathered by the sweep could be used as the base for 'pikes' (tall rounded heaps) which could be left out in the fields to weather for weeks before being led in.

Again for Ray's benefit, John has built some pikes, drawing on his memory of 50 or more years ago. One forkload of hay follows another as the heap rises to about 10 feet. Then the long-handled forks are used to pat it into shape. To prevent hay from blowing off the top of the pike, it's secured by ropes tied to balls of hay which are thrust into the base of the rick. The final touch is to rake up the loose hay all round the foot of the pike and then kick in the base to make sure it's firm – and looks neat. In pike-building, as in everything else, there was a right way and a wrong way to do it. And the look of the finished object was almost as important as its strength.

Carting pikes back to the farm was done on low-loader trailer called a bogey, hauled by a single horse in shafts. This forms the subject for the fourth of Ray's sculptures. The hay bogey (also called 'rick lifter') was an implement with an ingeniously simple winching device. It was backed into the side of a pike, and its platform tipped at an angle suitable for sliding under the hay. A chain was then wrapped round the base of the pike and fixed to a bar which was wound round and round by a windlass. This dragged the pike onto the platform of the bogey. As the hay was pulled into place, the platform gently fell back into position. It was important to make sure the pike was positioned in the centre of the bogey, because invariably the route home went through gates and there was a risk the load would catch on the gateposts and slip off.

The horse rake, fifth in Ray Ayres's new series of models, was an integral feature on British farms from about 1875. Drawn by a single horse in shafts, these rakes were used to clean all the remaining wisps of hay from a field at the end of the haymaking period. The most popular were eight feet wide with 24 curved teeth for gathering the hay. The driver waited until the rake was full and then kicked a foot pedal or pulled a lever. This raised the teeth, leaving behind a pile of hay.

Hay rakes were fast, mobile implements

and they were often drawn by a light horse rather than a Shire or a Clydesdale. Because of the rakes' apparent simplicity, farmers sometimes let boys or women operate them. But there could be tragic consequences. 'My father used to tell the same story until I was pig sick of hearing it,' John remembers. 'It was about a young woman raking hay. Her horse went over a wasp's nest and bolted. She fell off and was trailed across the field in the hay rake. Normally if something gets fast in a hayrake it lifts up. But it didn't lift up in her case and she was killed. I once asked an old horseman if he'd ever been on a hayrake when the horse bolted and he said he had. The only thing to do was try and hang on to your seat, because the horse would have to stop somewhere. But it had been a terrifying experience.'

Ray Ayres has seen a range of haymaking machines working in their natural environment. It's been a lesson in living history for him. He walks back to the farm with John, Richard and Norman, while David brings a pike back on a bogey. It'll be forked into a hayloft above one of the cow byres. Ray is inspired to go back to his studio and continue developing his models. At this early stage he works in wax and regularly turns up at Sillywrea with pale, half-finished figurines, seeking a word of advice on a detail he's concerned about.

He altered the look of the two horses pulling the grass mower after a suggestion from David. 'I felt one of the horses was looking the wrong way,' says David. 'It would have been more natural for it to be looking at the uncut grass because it would be wanting to eat some, rather than the other way. It's just a simple thing but it's flattering to think that Ray listens to us.'

Ray is only too happy to listen to their views. 'John's comment about the hay bogey and pike was that the hay on the model was too shallow and needed building up,' says Ray. 'And that's what I'm working on at the moment. We've been discussing the wheels on the bogey, and a couple of points about the harness. I've taken his views on board.

'He also doesn't want the horse to rush, so I have to make it look as though it's taking it steady. It's just another load of hay and there'll be plenty more to come. That's the feeling the model needs to convey. That's John's view: the horse's pace is important if you're going to do the job properly.

'Our models are noted for the amount of detail they contain. But obviously from a manufacturing point of view I can't design models that are too fragile. I have to make some compromises. They are as authentic as we can possibly make them, given the limitations of the material we work in.'

Shearing Time

In rural areas, harvesting food from field or hedgerow has always been a part of life, whether it's blackberries in August, mushrooms in September, crab apples in October, or sloes (for making into sloe gin) in November. In June and July, elder bushes have always been seen as a bountiful source of nourishment: the dark berries are delicious in pies and make wonderful jam, while the cream heads are an essential ingredient in elderflower champagne. Made with sugar and yeast, many bottles of this refreshing drink are brewed during the summer, bubbling quietly on the stone slabs in farmhouse pantries – and sometimes exploding with alarmingly loud cracks when the heady mixture gets too strong.

You may shear your sheep
When the elder blossoms peep

It's the elder blossom that ushers in the season for clipping time at Sillywrea. Shearing a sheep is a necessary ritual because it removes old wool and encourages new growth. And (until recent times) wool also constituted an important crop. Wool is the commodity that brought prosperity to landowners and yeoman farmers throughout the Middle Ages. More fundamentally, it provided the basic material for clothing.

Clipping days on upland farms were a communal activity, much enjoyed by everyone. Farmers and their workers travelled from farm to farm, helping neighbours with the time-consuming task of shearing their ewes and rams. Clipping has to be done in good weather, when the fleeces are dry, so as soon as a fine spell began the sheep were gathered into small fields near the farm for the big day. In summer, sheep were mostly out on higher ground, with the lowland fields shut off for hay. There weren't many places to hold a large number of sheep awaiting the shearers. The quicker the clipping was done, the better.

With their hand-shears, regularly whetted

on stones, farmers and shepherds could work their way through 20 sheep every hour. Shears in some districts were handed down as heirlooms from father to son, the leather pouches they were slotted into engraved with the initials of the original owner. Usually shearers bend over their sheep, in a posture that became backbreaking as the day progressed, particularly for a tall man. In some hill farming areas the clipper sat astride a narrow bench called a 'sheep form' and sheared the ewe as she lay writhing on the bench in front of him, head tucked under his arm. Trying not to cut too close and nick the skin, nor too far from the body and leave the best wool behind, shearers had to develop the knack of removing the wool in one piece. As it fell to the floor, a 'wrapper' (often a child) would roll the fleece and tie it with a piece of wool teased from the fleece, before placing the greasy bundle in a woolsack. Sometimes there was a sheet spread over the floor to catch all the clippings, especially the 'daggs' – dung-caked bits of wool from around the sheep's tail. At one time, even this soiled wool had a market. Often wrappers were also 'catchers' – delegated to surge into the pens and drag out the next struggling sheep for the men to clip. All this frenzied activity went on to the sound of sheep bleating, dogs barking and the snip-snip-snip of shears. Regular cries of 'Mark!' punctuated the air. This was a signal for the wrapper to stamp a freshly-clipped sheep with the farm's own distinctive 'pop' mark, often the farmer's initials. This had to be done at the same place on the flank of every sheep. Together with notches on ears and marks burned into horns, pop marks provided a way of identifying every sheep on the unfenced northern hills, a system which continues to this day. Shepherds' 'meets' are held in villages in summer and autumn at which stray sheep are gathered together and their identity established using the *Shepherd's Guide*, an annual publication which lists the markings of every sheep on every hill farm. First launched in the Lake District nearly 200 years ago this guide has proved to be an essential handbook for northern farmers.

Feeding a crowd of clippers and helpers was a challenge for the farmer's wife who would spend days beforehand baking bread, pies and cakes for the men. The clipping, part of the age-old cycle of sheep farming, carried with it a sense of celebration. When the day was done there'd be dancing and singing, fuelled by ale specially brewed for the occasion.

'No doubt they'd have a great day out and enjoy the get-together,' John says, smiling at the thought of it. 'I've heard tell of the days when Sillywrea used to help out at Harsondale, the next farm, at clipping time. But since I began work on the farm, we've not got involved with other people's shearing days. It's always been more of a tradition on the real hill farms, whereas we seem to be somewhere in the middle. Neither a really hard upland farm, nor a fertile lowland farm.'

Until David joined him John clipped his flock himself, using hand shears in the traditional way He liked to clip in Race Week, the last week of June, when Newcastle Races are held, culminating with the Northumberland Plate on the Saturday. Ideally, haymaking would start the following week. 'I was never a fast clipper,' he says. 'About 50 a day was my limit. I would clip and Frances would catch and wrap. We had fewer sheep then, so I just took it steady. Then one year I had a bad back, so we got the shearing contractors in. And we've had them ever since. They're a lot faster than me or David. They can shear a sheep like peeling an orange.'

Even the system of marking his sheep has changed. Neither Cheviots nor Suffolks have horns, so there's nowhere to burn a horn mark on them. And 'lug marks' (on the sheep's ears) have been superceded by tags which show the animal's age and its farm of origin. 'No doubt it's a good thing for keeping track of sheep,' John says. 'Everyone seems to have a lot more sheep than they used to these days.'

Until the beginning of the 20th century, sheep were often washed in a local river or stream a couple of days before clipping. In some places this meant building a sizable dam in a mountain stream to make a big enough pool for farmers and their staff to stand up to their waists in water, ducking their animals to get rid of the worst of the winter's dirt. The fleece lost weight as some of the grease was washed out, but 'clean' wool fetched a bigger price at that time so it was reckoned to be worth the effort.

John recalls hearing his father reminiscing about washing the sheep in the River Allen half a mile from Sillywrea. 'There was a proper pool and the sheep were put in and made to swim to the other side,' he says. 'While it paid to do it, because of a higher price for the wool, they kept it up. But eventually it wasn't worth all the effort that it involved.'

Haymaking

With Ray Ayres gone, David and John return to the hay. One of their few concessions to today's farming methods is to use a tractor-driven baler to package the crop. With only Norman to help them, it would be physically impossible to build 50 acres of hay into pikes and lead them one by one back to the farm. The weather is notoriously unpredictable, too, so it's better to use a machine which can parcel up hay quickly. They've resorted to borrowing or hiring a tractor, which David drives, and a baler. It's not a modern machine, though. Big round bales wouldn't fit with a horse-based system. The baler they use was popular on farms in the 1960s and 1970s. It produces small oblong bales, knotted together by two strings and gathered by a sledge towed behind the machine.

In pre-Second World War farming, when there were plenty of hands to make the hay, everyone stayed all day in the hayfield. Supplies of food and drink were brought to the workers at regular intervals. A snack at eleven

213

o'clock or three, perhaps. Or larger picnics at dinnertime (noon) or teatime (quarter to four). A servant lass would walk out to the field carrying a huge wicker basket groaning with sandwiches, buns, pies, cakes and pots of tea. The horses would sometimes be 'loosed out' of the haymaking machines and stood in the shade. A white cloth would be spread out on the hay, the men would prop their forks or rakes against the hedge and the food would be handed round. In some parts of the north, farmers provided their workers with home-brewed beer, partly because it stimulated them to work faster – and home-brewed was cheaper than bought-in beer. At Sillywrea, however, they stuck to tea.

By remaining wedded to using small bales, John and David have kept open the door for casual workers to lend a hand at haytime. Big bales can only be wrapped in plastic bags by machine; they can only be shifted by tractor. But small bales can be manhandled by anyone who doesn't mind the strings cutting into their fingers. Rather than being left lying flat where they would soak up moisture, the bales are propped into 'stooks' to continue maturing in the field before eventually being led in by horse-drawn bogey. 'Stooking' is a term which goes back to the days of corn harvesting by sickle, when newly cut sheaves were propped against one another to dry. Stooked hay bales may be the product of a tractor-driven machine, but they are still an unusual sight in the countryside today. Technology has moved on so fast that what was current on farms 30 years ago is now virtually obsolete.

Among the people who like to help out with the hay is computer programmer Ed Brown. He's been pitching in at Sillywrea for about 20 years. 'I've known the family for a long time and it's important to me to give them a hand when they're busy in the hay. I tell John when I'm available and he calls me when he needs me. I like it. It's satisfying.' Along with other friends and acquaintances of John and David's he's part of a regular gang dedicated to stooking bales in the field. But he's also happy to volunteer to be in the hayloft receiving the bales hoisted up by elevator – even though the stacked hay gives off a huge amount of heat and it's warm, thirsty work. 'It's a different way of life, it's a good deal more relaxed than I'm used to. In my own job, I work by myself and all I've got to show for it is a little floppy disk. Here, you're part of a team doing something you won't come across anywhere else in the country. You're achieving something and at the end of the day you feel it's been worth it.'

Keeping Ed and other helpers busy in the barn are Norman and David, each with a horse and hay bogey. While one's unloading the bales onto the wooden slats of the elevator, the other's fetching another load. Stacking a bogey is a skill. Light, early season hay has a slipperiness which could lead to losing a load on a sloping field or over ruts. The bottom row of bales should be laid on their side for better grip, with the next layer placed the opposite way for strength. Three or four courses (25–30 bales) is enough for the horse to pull on 'short leads' – loads from fields close to the farm. For longer leads, a slightly larger load, even more carefully packed, is possible as long as the horse pulling the bogey takes its time.

'There's a temptation to rush at things in haytime because you're always up against the weather,' John says. 'I can only remember one summer when we weren't battling with showers of rain and that was 1976. It was just myself at the time – Frances was at college – and I cut 60 acres and made it into hay in 3 weeks. I was hardly ever abed. At nights and weekends I got a lot of help to bring the hay in, but we'd be leading hay until 11 o'clock. The rest of the time I was on my own.'

He adds drily, winking at his wife: 'It was the first time I knew Maggie thought much of me. She was fair in tears one morning. I was getting out of bed at four o'clock and she says: "You'll kill yourself."

'I says to her: "There'll be plenty of time when the hay is won!"'

Restoration

Martin Jackson contemplates the huge ash tree trunk sprawling in a corner of his depot on the outskirts of Hexham in Northumberland. 'Aye,' he says. 'A fine tree. No doubt about that.' The timber merchant has been combing his yard for a special piece of wood for his friend John Dodd. From the huge mass of the 150-year-old tree lying before him will be fashioned new shafts for one of John's horse-drawn trailers. It has to be wood that will last a lifetime.

Now in his eighties, Martin isn't as active in the timber trade as he used to be. His son Michael runs the business. But Martin's still involved in buying trees. He's almost sure the ash has come from the Whitfield estate, which lies only a few miles from John's farm. It has forests on the flanks of the Pennine hills. Constantly buffeted by winds, the trees grow up in harsh surroundings. Toughness is a component of their make-up.

The ash tree was felled in the winter and brought by lorry to the yard where it has lain seasoning for nine months. Martin knows from personal experience what the wood should be like for the task that lies ahead. He spent the first 16 years of his life on the land. His most vivid memory revolves round the family 'flitting' (moving farms) in 1931 when he was just 10. He was given an important job to do: walk in front of the family's flock of sheep as they meandered seven miles along a series of country roads to a new farm they were renting. This was quite a responsibility for a boy. He was placed there partly to stop the animals stringing out in a long line, and partly to warn other road users they were coming. Another boy with a couple of dogs drove them from behind. 'I must have been tired by the time we got to the new place,' he says. 'But I've never forgotten that day.'

Not that the Jacksons stayed there all that

long. It was during the agricultural depression of the inter-war years, when low prices drove many people off the land. Martin's father was forced to quit his farm in 1936 and go back to working in the woods, which had been his first calling. But those 16 years on a farm have stood Martin in good stead. 'Ash is best for shafts,' he says. 'It's strong but lighter than oak. We always used to make shafts out of ash in the old days.'

On the wall of the timber yard office are some yellowing photographs of men working in the woods long ago. In one of them, two heavy horses yoked in line strain to heave a wood-waggon down a rough forest track. The waggon is loaded with knobbly ash trees.

'Before the Second World War, when there was a lot of labour available, we used to use horses quite a lot to pull trees out of the wood. And we had steam engines driving the sawmill. But life moves on. Tractors replaced horses and electric power took over from steam in the sawmill.

'When we started off we used to provide a lot of timber for all the collieries in the area. Pit props were needed for the narrow seams. Then the coal-mines closed and we looked for other markets. For a while there was a market for timber with all the new roads that were going through: motorway fencing, that kind of thing. But as well as this we've always gone out of our way to cater for all the farmers round about, making sheep troughs and gates, or anything else they might need.

'We class ourselves as a country sawmill. We've always bought our timber from local estates. Places within a 30-mile radius. That way, you know the trees and you know where they grew.'

Industrial loaders bustle backwards and forwards, moving raw timber round the yard. Cranes tower overhead. Loads of softwood such as Scots pine, Norway spruce and larch arrive on massive lorries. There are heaps of firewood, mountains of pallets and piles of sawn logs. Everything is on a large scale, but Martin doesn't mind helping the small customer.

'The farm where I grew up was at Langley, not far from John Dodd's farm. I knew his father. We've kept in touch and been friendly over the years. If you're from a farm you're always interested in farm work. And if you grew up with farm horses, it's something you never lose. I still like to give people a hand if they've got horses.'

John's first memory of Martin is a colourful one. 'He took me and a distant relation, Billy

Dodd, ratting one night.' On a moonlit night hunting rats with sticks was a sport which gripped many youngsters – and it usually had the approval of the grown-ups. In some villages there was a vermin paymaster who offered a bounty of a penny a tail. 'Farms in those days seemed to be teeming with rats and the damage they did was immense. We were just lads and we had a grand time.'

As his timber business grew, Martin took on a man who used to deliver logs round Hexham with a horse and cart. On one occasion, needing a new horse, Martin contacted John to see if he would sell him one. 'I didn't have anything that would have suited him at the time,' says John, 'so I took him to a dealer at Penrith, Watson Iveson of Pooley Bridge, and he got a very good mare from him. That horse lasted a long time and did a good job for Martin and we've been friendly ever since.'

John and David have called in at the timber yard to discuss the making of the new shafts. First, they need the wood. They watch from a distance as a loader grabs the specially selected ash tree in its jaws and deposits it on a conveyor. This feeds it into the sawmill. Emitting a high-pitched whine, a blade slices the tree into planks four inches thick which trundle on rollers out of the far side of the mill. David and John, helped by the yard foreman, carry the rough-hewn piece of wood into the joiner's shop, where it will be cut to size. They're sweating as they lay it on the bench. 'There's some weight in that plank,' John says, wiping his brow. 'Took a bit of carrying. In the old days they reckoned all a farmer needed to be was strong o' the back and thick o' the head. There may be some truth in it. But I'm not as strong as I used to be!'

The horsemen have brought an old pair of shafts to guide the joiner when he's cutting out the new ones. They lay the shafts on top of the plank, so he can see where to cut. Various points are mentioned. Tape measures are produced. Martin Jackson promises he'll be available for advice if he's needed. He says: 'You have to have a pattern to work from when you're making shafts. It's the shape that varies. Some have one bend in them, some two bends. They can vary quite a lot, depending on what machine they come from.'

The joiner, Brian Lowdon, takes his pencil from behind his ear and starts to sketch some lines on the wood. John and David announce that it's time to go. 'We'll leave you chaps to it,' John says. 'Give us a call when they're ready.' And with that, they manoeuvre their pickup out of the yard and head for home.

A few weeks later David collects the newly made shafts from the sawmill, but six months pass before he and his father-in-law get round to fitting them. They are destined to be fixed to an old bogey which the two men are restoring. Bogeys are broad, low trailers pulled by a single horse. Mostly used for carrying hay or straw, they were known as rullies or rollies in other parts of the country.

John outlines the history of this particular bogey, which in these days of built-in obsolescence is another example of the astonishing durability of joiner-made horse-drawn machinery. It is, literally, an antique. The original was made by a carpenter called Robson from the village of Matfen, north-east of Hexham, in the early years of the 20th century. 'My father was born in 1899 and he could remember being just a schoolboy when my grandfather came home with a new bogey – and this is it, still going strong!' New boards were fitted to it in 1940, but the soles (beams) and cross-over spars are the original parts.

John says: 'It was lying about the farm and we couldn't decide what to do about it. The top was rotten and the wheels had gone west but it was a little too good to break up for firewood, so we decided to see if we could restore it.

'Renovating these old things grows on you, it's something you enjoy. You're using the knowledge and experience you've gained over a lifetime. I was reluctant to leave the farm as a boy because I was so keen on the horses but the twelvemonth I spent as a joiner's apprentice has come in useful after all this time. For all it's nearly 60 years ago, the wood-working skills I learned then keep coming back.'

David feels the same: 'I enjoy working with old machines. The wood is often rotted away and the working parts may be all rusted up, but you can see the potential in them. Getting them going again is a challenge I enjoy. It's a rotational thing, having a collection of farm implements. You try and maintain two or three of every type because you never know what might happen. You might get a puncture at haytime and not have time to fix it, so it pays to have a bogey or two in reserve.

'I just like seeing everything completed as it should be when we renovate something. There's a sense of pride when we've done the job right. Here, we are trying to make a bogey which is functional as well as being faithful to the original.'

The men are aware that if their time was properly costed out at contemporary joiners' rates, the bogey could be considered an expensive piece of equipment. But John adds: 'It's a job you can always do on a wet afternoon when you can't get on the land. It fills the time in.'

In earlier days hay bogeys ran on two wooden or iron wheels. John recalls with affection the products of a Northumberland firm, Simms of Newton, which was famous for its agricultural machinery, particularly grass-cutters. But Simms also made top-notch bogeys with fine wooden wheels.

Most of the later models had rubber tyres. This gave John and David an almost insurmountable problem when they were half-way through the restoration. 'The wheels are just about unique,' David says. 'They're the same size as the wheels on the wartime Spitfire fighter planes, but, as you can imagine, they're not making many of those any more. It's hard finding the valves and tubes. People wonder what you're on about when you start asking for aeroplane tyres – especially when they know you're just a farmer! So we've had to scout around the district to try and find some wheels, and eventually we were successful.'

The new shafts were a few inches longer than the original ones. John explains: 'A horse was apt to catch its hocks on the frame on the old bogey because the shafts were just a shade too short. It meant the animal was pulling, as we say it, by the back bands rather than the shoulder chains. In other words it was putting a strain on the horse.'

With the shafts finally fixed in place at the front of the bogey, David and John turn their attention to the body. The sawmill has cut them a pile of six-inch-wide larch boards for the floor, and there's the harsh din of hammering as they are nailed into place. Painting the frame red completes the restoration. The men stand back to admire their work. 'We like to give an implement a lick of paint when we've finished restoring it,' David says. 'On a working farm like this it doesn't last long. You soon knock the edges off it. But that moment when you've given it the final coat of paint and it looks as good as new, well, you can imagine what it must have looked like when it came from the joiner's shop almost a hundred years ago.'

Autumn

Harvest

At Sillywrea, as on any farm where corn is grown, harvest is a crucial time. In ancient days, a poor harvest meant starvation, and while nothing so drastic would happen in the developed world today, farmers still cast anxious eyes at the skies as the time approaches to cut their cereal crops.

These days the retail price of a top-of-the-range combine harvester is not far short of £200,000, but it is the ultimate labour-saving machine. It has an output of more than 60 tonnes of grain an hour and in the right conditions, it can cut 100 acres of corn a day. A farm with 2000 acres of oilseed rape, beans, wheat and barley ripening in succession could harvest the lot with that one machine. With modern 110-horsepower tractors costing in the region of £50,000 it means that to equip such a farm with a full range of modern machinery could cost £500,000.

What a contrast to the corn harvests of the early 19th century! There were no noisy machines to cut the crop, no line of tractors and trailers waiting for the grain, no clouds of dust. Instead the fields thronged with people, all engaged in unremitting toil. First came the reaper armed with his sickle, a tool little changed since the Iron Age. With its serrated cutting edge (in the north it was known as the 'toothed hewk'), the sickle was drawn through the standing corn close to the ground, severing the stems and leaving the stubble behind. As the corn fell in even rows behind the reapers, it was gathered into sheaves and tied with a straw 'rope' or band. This was made by taking a handful of corn, splitting it in two and tying the heads together in a simple knot. Often this part of the harvesting was done by women. In some areas where large arable farms abounded, these women were known as 'bondagers' because they had to be supplied by the farm labourers.

When the ground had been cleared of cut corn the sheaves were propped up against each other to dry. The number of sheaves in these 'stooks' varied from area to area. Ten was a common number, but in some areas it was more. A 'thrave' or 'threave' was two stooks of 12 sheaves each. The word is still used in some places to mean 'two dozen'.

The stooks dried best when they were put up in lines running east to west to get the maximum benefit from the sun.

The speed of working rose or fell according to the ripeness of the crop and the skill of the reapers. It was estimated that, using sickles, a team of three could reap, bind and stook an acre of grain on a good day.

Traditionally, the stooks stayed in the field for three Sundays to allow the corn to dry out. Then they were transported back to the farm. Once again, even loading a cart, a waggon or a trailer was a recognised skill. Usually one man forked the sheaves and another, who was more experienced, built the load. The butts (cut ends of the stems) were always on the outside, with the heads of corn sloping down towards the centre. This helped to prevent the load from sliding off.

In many districts the last sheaf to leave the field was given special attention in a ritual which had distinctly pagan origins. To preserve the 'Corn Spirit' and ensure a good harvest the following year, this sheaf was ceremonially wrapped in ribbons and paraded aloft on the final load. This is the origin of the corn or kirn 'dollies', traditional decorations woven from straw which are still sold in craft shops throughout the country.

In many arable areas, when the last waggon had left for the farm it was a signal for women and children to move in and glean the fields, picking up any shed ears of corn from the stubble and putting them into sacks. They fed these free gleanings to their hens, or ground them into flour.

For centuries the main device used to separate the grain from the ears was the flail, usually an ash shank to the end of which a shorter piece of wood was attached by a thong. Sheaves were spread on a threshing floor (often in the granary) to be beaten with flails. Once the corn had been threshed the chaff (husks) still had to be removed in a process called winnowing. The term comes from Old English 'windwain' meaning wind. It involves directing a draught of air through and over the grain as it's being stirred by a winnower wielding a shallow dish. The aim is to waft away the husks.

In upland areas this was sometimes done on the first floor of stone barns which had doors on two sides. When both doors were open, a current would blow through the barn taking the chaff with it.

A number of developments in the 1800s transformed the laborious process of harvesting as it had been carried out for centuries. First on the scene was the horse-drawn reaper, which cut the corn and left it in swathes behind the machine. Labourers were still needed to bind the corn into sheaves, however, and the search continued for a machine that could take mechanical harvesting a stage further. Agricultural engineers realised that they could be on the brink of a massive new market, and many worked on their inventions in secret – even harvesting crops of wheat at the dead of night in clandestine attempts to test their new machines without them being spotted (and copied) by someone else.

By the 1880s the corn reaper was being replaced by the reaper-binder, which did everything except thresh the crop. It was one of the most sophisticated machines of all. Revolving wooden paddles (which looked like the sails of a windmill) forced the corn against a cutter-bar with V-shaped knife sections which went from side to side at high speed. The cut corn fell in even rows onto a platform. From there it was carried between two canvas belts before being separated into sheaves and bound with twine by a knotter. Then it was spat out of the back of the binder to be gathered into stooks.

Farm labourers, marvelling at the speed

and efficiency of the binder, used to joke that the knotter was a device of such ingenuity that it wasn't surprising that the person who dreamed it up had ended up in a lunatic asylum. They used to look at the knotter and say: 'Only a tortured mind could have invented that!'

At Sillywrea, the first time a binder made its appearance was 1940. From having never grown a blade of corn, the farm, like many others, was now under orders to produce grain as part of the country's Dig for Victory campaign. Forty acres of barley were harvested. 'To begin with my father hired a contractor with a binder to cut the corn, but after I got started with the horses we bought a binder and I cut it with the horses. Three horses abreast pulling a Massey-Harris binder. Oh, it was a lovely job cutting corn – if the weather was fine and things were going right. The strange thing was you'd do all the harvest work after dinner because at that time of the year there were heavy dews in the mornings. It seemed that you could do a tremendous lot of harvest work after dinner whereas you never seemed to do as much hay work after dinner. I don't know why it was, but that's the way I remember it.'

While John cut the corn, his father stooked the sheaves, helped on some occasions by Maggie's brother Harold, who worked part-time at Sillywrea, and on others by an Irish labourer who would be hired for the harvest. 'It was a nice job stooking corn when you started, but it was sickening by the time you finished. We always made stooks with 10 sheaves – they used to stand best that way. One pair straight up in the middle and two pairs on each side sloping in a little. Of course if it came to a lot of bad weather you had to start shifting the stooks, or the corn in the heads would start to grow and the tops would get all matted together.'

Binders were heavy machines which could be hard on the horses. In wet harvests the main land wheel which drove all the working parts would skid along the ground and the cutterbar and canvases would get choked. John can recall some atrocious weather years: '54 was a bad 'un. Got the corn cut with a binder, but didn't lead the last load in until the sixth of November.'

But other years, harvest was plain sailing. John has happy memories of clear, breezy nights when they'd lead the sheaves in until it got dark. Sometimes they'd even continue in moonlight.

235

When it was brought home to the farm, the corn was stored in stacks (ricks). On many farms, these were built on a foundation of branches, supposedly to keep the bottom layer dry, but at Sillywrea they didn't use branches because it was felt they provided a nesting space for rats. Even more care was lavished on constructing stacks than was spent on building the cartloads of sheaves that came in from the cornfields. The stacker worked on his knees laying one layer of sheaves clockwise and the next layer anti-clockwise. Stacks were barrel-shaped, and the sheaves were laid sloping slightly to the outside so that when it rained the water didn't run in but dripped off. The sides were shaped with a scythe blade or a pair of shears to give a neat appearance, and the roof was properly thatched. 'They used to say a good stacker didn't need to thatch his stack, but they were better if they were,' John says. Thatching was done with painstaking care. Nets were available to make the roof more secure, but many of the older men wouldn't countenance them. They liked to decorate their stacks with a straw ornament – often a bird like a pheasant, or an animal like a fox. 'The best I ever did was wind some corn into a knob and fix it to the top,' John recalls.

Even that would have invited comment. Like much else in farming at a time when appearances seemed to count more than they do today, the ricks standing in a stack-yard were scrutinised by all and sundry, and caustic were the remarks if they leaned one way or another, had a swollen 'belly', or had holes in their thatching.

What the corn stacks were waiting for was threshing day – another communal activity enjoyed by farmers everywhere. Threshing took place at any time between October and April, and was invariably an event which, like clipping day, needed extensive preparations. Extra hands had to be found to carry out the many tasks – and cooking and baking went on for weeks before to lay up supplies of food to feed the men.

Historians credit a Scot named Andrew Meikle for inventing the machine which catapulted threshing from the age of the flail and winnowing fan into the era of steam. As early as 1786 Meikle developed a thresher which battered the grain from the heads of corn and separated the straw, and in 1800 he added a winnowing device to remove the chaff. It would be another 70-odd years before a mobile version of his prototype would become a common visitor to farms throughout Britain, however.

At Sillywrea the corn was threshed over four days during the winter. Workers were needed to fork the sheaves up to the thresher platform, cut the bands (strings), bag the grain and clear away the chaff and straw. 'You had to have a minimum of 12 men but it was better if you had 14,' says John. 'You wanted to get cleaned up, otherwise what happened is you'd get a windy night and everything would blow all over the place. After a few years it got harder and harder to hire a thresher, so I bought one.

'Eventually, in 1970, we stopped cutting corn with a binder and threshing it with a thresher. The small amount of corn we have now is cut by a contractor with a combine harvester. It's the only way. There aren't the people left to stook sheaves, lead corn, stack it and thresh it. Those days have gone.'

Threshing was dirty work. People's faces were coated in dust and they drank copious amounts of cold tea to slake their thirsts. It was a noisy, often monotonous job dominated by the pounding of the steam engine and the never-ending slapping of long belts which stretched from the engine to the thresher and drove the machine.

But John has some vivid memories – good

and bad – of the time when threshing days were at their peak. Carrying corn in bags could be an ordeal. The sacks were often too heavy (wheat was kept in sacks weighing 16 stone), and struggling up the steps to a granary was difficult. Few steps had railings, as they would have to have under today's safety rules. 'I was going up some wooden steps one day with a bag when the steps gave way. I crashed down and the corn cascaded onto the ground. The farmer rushed out to see what had happened. But it wasn't me he was concerned about – he wanted to know why the corn had been spilled!'

There was humour – and there were some hair-raising moments. One year John helped out at a nearby farm where the corn was being threshed by a contractor called Emerson Bowman. Emerson, used to drawn-out haggling with his customers over the price of a day's work, was a cool-headed, inscrutable man who wasn't easily fazed. Until this particular threshing day, that is. John recalls the moment with vivid clarity. 'A rat appeared out of the stack, and by goodness it was a big one. Two chaps were trying to fell it, and a terrier was after it. But it was too quick for them. Emerson should have had his trouser legs fastened with string. But he hadn't...'

Seeing a place to hide, the rat disappeared up the thresher man's trouser leg and came to a stop on his hip. Everyone around stood and gaped at the huge squirming bulge. 'Eukh,' says John, shuddering and laughing at the same time. 'Just imagine what it must have felt like, wriggling and scratching inside your trousers. What a terrible feeling.'

But Emerson had a reputation to maintain. 'He kept very calm,' John recalls. 'Very slowly, he took off his things. First his cap and then his specs, then his jacket and his pullover. And when he pulled his shirt up the rat came out with the shirt – and then scuttled back down into his trousers!'

It was more a case of wait-and-see than cat-and-mouse. Emerson, now bare-chested, could still feel the rat burrowing backwards and forwards in his trousers. After what seemed an age, it peeped over the belt-hoops, and jumped out and scampered away. 'Emerson may have looked calm, but he was as white as a sheet,' John chuckles. 'He was very lucky he didn't get bitten.'

In 1851 there were 1,480,000 agricultural workers in England and Wales, a figure which had fallen by half 100 years later, and today stands at around 100,000. The threshing machine, followed by the combine harvester, have played their own remorseless role in the steady decline of the farm workforce.

Shire Horse Sale

Like many of his generation, John hasn't travelled far. On a farm where there are animals, you can't be away for too long. Livestock need feeding and watering. You worry that something may go wrong while you're away. The furthest places John has ventured to are Oban on the west coast of Scotland (for a cattle sale), Edinburgh (to the auction mart), Blackpool (for a horse sale) and Scarborough (for a day out). So David is surprised when his father-in-law agrees to accompany him to a sale in East Yorkshire. It's one of the longest trips of his life, but it promises to be a special one.

For 18 years Flower Hill Farm at North Newbold near Market Weighton was the home of the Northern Shire Horse Centre. This tourist attraction boasted a fine collection of horses, a range of original stables, a museum of country life, a harness room, a farmhouse kitchen and a working forge. It was popular with visitors from all over the country. But eventually the owner, Bill Cammidge, reached the age where he wanted to take things easy. He'd been a horseman in his youth and broken in many horses. When tractors came along he'd kept his Shires as a hobby and gradually built up his collection of horse equipment. The museum had been a success, but sadly his son and grandson didn't want to carry on. So the time had come for the centre to close. Everything was up for sale: 15 pedigree Shire horses, a range of horse-drawn implements, a vast collection of horse harness and some vintage tractors and engines. It was the end of an era.

David and John decide it's too good to miss. Sandwiches packed in a basket and Thermos full of tea, they set off in the pickup for another day at the sales.

As soon as they arrive, the Northumberland farmer and his son-in-law realise there probably won't be any bargains. The auctioneers, Hornsey and Sons, have advertised the event far and wide and a huge number of people have turned up. Many are here out of curiosity to be sure, but looking at the expensive vehicles lined up in the car park John and David know there's plenty of money around. 'Still,' John says, 'I'm glad we've come. It's a sad day when a place like this closes down. You never know. If we keep our eyes and ears open we might get something.'

In the days when horses still dominated on farms, the Shire was the most popular breed in England and Wales. The tallest in the world and considerably larger than the Clydesdale, it was the ultimate workhorse – slow, dignified and even-tempered. It had strength, stamina and an infinite capacity to adapt to new working situations. At one time there were large numbers of bay, grey or black Shires dragging barges along canals, pulling brewer's drays from pub to pub and hauling trains in cities. Where power was needed, people turned to the Shire.

But, like all heavy horses, Shires have declined steeply. Numbers plummeted after the end of the Second World War. The closure of the Northern Shire Horse Centre is another nail in their coffin.

Flower Hill is a traditional Yorkshire Wolds farm renowned for growing bountiful crops of wheat, barley, peas and sugar beet on south-facing land which slopes into a deep, dry valley. It's 25 September and the harvest is long over. A field of stubble provides a tan-coloured backdrop against which the museum's horse-drawn implements and other vintage machines are displayed in rows. Overhead, a vast blue sky is broken up by fleecy clouds. The air is still. It's a perfect autumn day.

A century ago, when wheelwrights were in their prime and joiners prided themselves in their handiwork, farm carts differed in design from area to area. Three distinctly different carts are up for sale, from Yorkshire, Cheshire and the Fens. There are two brewer's drays, a shooting brake and a vehicle for exercising a pair of horses. A giant Foster steam threshing machine towers over turnip slicers, harrows, ploughs, hay turners, rakes, rollers and cultivators. At the centre of it all is a beautiful Wolds waggon built in the 19th century by Sissons the wheelwrights, of Beverley. It's painted in the traditional colour of yellow with a red-and-blue lining and red wheels.

These are all items which generations of farmers and farm labourers, most of them no longer with us, will have used day in, day out for years. Part of our past, they have at least been saved from the scrapyard. Now they're about to move on to new homes.

It's already midday and John and David only have time for a cursory look round the horse-drawn implements. In sharp contrast to the offerings at Healey Mill, the sale they went to in July everything here looks in good condition. John makes a mental note of the machines that might be useful to him. He's mildly interested in a fertiliser spreader. It's the same make as one he's already got at Sillywrea, but as the remaining number of such machines dwindles and the supply of spare parts disappears altogether, it's always worth having a second machine waiting in the wings. The problem about buying machines at a sale so far from home, John knows, is getting them back to the farm without paying more for transport than he's forked out for the machine. David's noticed that the farm manager from Beamish Museum in County Durham is among the crowd. Maybe he has a lorry.

A bell rings out and within minutes the auctioneer has launched into his robust selling repertoire, a mixture of dry Yorkshire humour and a breakneck cascade of words. A dozen soil-encrusted ploughshares of different sizes don't seem to be anything special but they fetch £35. Someone pays £75 for a collection of swingletrees. Both lots are far more than John would dream of paying. The signs are that it's going to be an expensive sale. But he's not deterred. His eye has fallen on three pairs of wooden shafts used for pulling light machines. To anyone else, they might seem worthless, but John knows how useful one of them would be at Sillywrea. As the crowd approaches John's spirits drop momentarily. He's spotted someone else he knows who might also be interested. 'He'll be trying to buy them for nothing, same as me,' he mutters gloomily, knowing that it only takes two people to want something badly enough for the bidding to career out of control. In the event, there's not a lot of competition for the shafts. The auctioneer only manages to coax a top bid of £50 from his audience and moves swiftly on to the next lot. John hasn't been bidding, but he's noted who bought the shafts. Within seconds, he's at the man's side. 'You wouldn't sell us one of those pairs of shafts?' he asks. The man's already bidding for something else, the merest hint of a wink indicating his interest to the auctioneer. Without turning to look at John he says: 'See us before you go.' There's no hiding John's amusement. It looks like he's going to get a bargain after all.

The vintage tractors due to come under the hammer include a 1948 Ferguson and a 1947 Field Marshall. It's a sad irony that, in their own way, these two machines will have contributed indirectly to the demise of the heavy horse, yet here they are at a Shire horse centre closing down sale, for all the world like traitors at a funeral. It's not surprising that John and David decide to miss this part of the proceedings. Instead, they go and look at the Shires. Two stallions, ten mares and three foals are tethered in stables and loose boxes in the Victorian farm buildings clustered round fold yards next to the farm house. They're superbly turned out, their coats glistening. Beautifully plaited into their manes are strands of red, white, blue and green wool. Jutting up are 'tips' or 'flights', pieces of coloured ribbon held erect by wires to form a nodding crest running from ears to withers. The skills involved in this decorative craft have been kept alive by the likes of Bill Cammidge and his family and when the horses are brought out to be sold there's a gasp of admiration from the waiting crowd. The Shires make a magnificent spectacle, trotting to and fro while bidders vie for the auctioneer's attention. John's captivated by the imposing presence of one of the stallions, Rook Hills Hercules, a dark bay 12-year-old who clearly lives up to his name. He weighs almost a ton. At 5 ft 5 inches, John's dwarfed by the huge animal, which measures almost six feet to the shoulders with another 20 inches to the top of his ears. 'Grand horse,' John says admiringly as he looks up at Hercules' noble head. 'Grand horse.'

The crowd meanders through the farm yard to a hayshed where harness is being sold. Heavy horses may be vanishing but there's clearly a market for harness – especially the decorated show harness resplendent with brass fittings. It makes more than £800. At the other end of the scale John and David bid for a rather worn work collar with metal hames. It goes for £45. They go after another in better condition, bidding it up before dropping out at £120. It sells for £220. 'You just have to keep your nerve,' John says. 'You'll regret it if you get carried away.'

David explains their bidding policy: 'We discuss it together and try to set a figure in our minds before we start bidding. We generally stick to our plan, but sometimes, because of competition from other trades, we're finding ourselves paying more and more for the things we require.'

Fortunately for them there are more collars on offer and their bid of £70 for one is successful. Then a horse blanket is knocked down to them for a few pounds.

As the sale nears its end John approaches the man who bought the shafts. He's a horse dealer from East Yorkshire, the type of person who might be looking to drive a hard bargain. But he recognises in John a fellow horse lover and after a brief moment of haggling, they agree a price. Then there's a minor stroke of luck. The blanket John and David bought didn't have a strap to fasten it. But the horse dealer's bought a job lot of half a dozen blanket straps and he lets John have one for next to nothing. John smiles broadly as he walks away from the sale, clutching his purchases. 'You can't beat the feeling that you've got a bargain or two,' he confides.

'It's been a marvellous sale,' John adds. 'There will be very few like this again. The harness was making too much money for the likes of us who are involved in everyday horse work. In a lot of cases the harness seemed to cost more than the horses. Some of those lots of harness were making a fantastic price and no doubt it's just collectors that are buying them. But all in all, it's been a great day out. I wouldn't have missed it for the world. I've never been here before, but this part of Yorkshire, it's great farming country. I could farm here if I'd been 50 years younger.'

Hauling Timber

Dawn on a late September day can sometimes bring a most extraordinary sight at Sillywrea: a whole field carpeted with gossamer. Money spiders have spent all night spinning their silken webs, and as the sun comes up there's a silver sheen on the surface of the meadow, broken in places by jagged lines where sheep have wandered. In a slight breeze, the webs shimmer in the sunlight like the rippling surface of the sea. The sheep look comical, seemingly oblivious of the wisps of white cobweb draped round their black muzzles as they munch the grass in their unhurried way. It's a scene which typifies autumn – John Dodd's favourite season. 'There's a time just after harvest when the countryside is looking wonderful,' he says. 'Sometimes you get an

Indian summer around that time and there's no better place to be.'

David is sauntering behind Davey through a countryside which is showing all the signs of a year in decline. Thistledown drifts gently across the fields. Beech leaves are turning golden. Willow herb stems blacken as the summer's life ebbs away.

Horse and man turn into a small wood. From ash tree branches hang bunches of the trees' fruit – pale clusters of dried seedpods rustling in the breeze. They're called 'keys' because of the way they resemble the instruments used to open medieval locks. Each has a single twisted wing which keeps it airborne as the winds take it spinning away from its parent tree to start a new life nearby.

Up through leaf litter and dead grass funghi push their fluted caps. The woodland boasts a colourful collection of mushrooms – free food for anyone who knows which are safe to collect.

But David has no plans to gather the fruits of autumn. He and Davey have some decidedly harder work to do.

Many old countrymen will tell you that it's going to be a severe winter when autumn brings an abundance of hips and haws. This year the hedgerows are bulging with rose hips (the fruit of the wild rose) and dark red hawthorn berries. If the old saying is right, it's all the more reason for David to lay in a larger than usual store of wood.

Trace chains stretch back from Davey's collar through loops in his leather back strap and loin straps. They're fastened to a metal swingletree, to which is connected a heavy dragging chain. This is for pulling timber out of the wood. 'We've eight acres of woodlands on the farm and there's a supply of firewood for ever more,' John explains. 'Frances and David burn a lot on open fires. But getting the trees out isn't easy. They're on a steep-sided place which tumbles down towards the river. The only way you can extract them is with a horse.'

Much of the wood is self-sown silver birch, which is now so far past maturity that many of the trees are rotten. David has been tidying up the wood by removing trees which are in danger of falling down. He's been doing that with one of the few contemporary machines on the farm, a chainsaw. Branches have been piled to one side and he's left with logs about 12 feet long. He winds the chain round the end of each log and fastens it with a large hook. 'C'mon little lad,' he says gently to his horse and off they go.

Forests are one of the very few places left in Britain where a small number of heavy horses still hold their own. Horsemen with Clydesdales or Shires are to be found working in woods in several areas. They have a supporting role to play in an industry increasingly dominated by machinery.

In 'clear-felling' an area of mature forest is cut to the ground, usually by giant machines that cut a tree and strip it of its branches in seconds. Once the area has been cleared it will be planted again. There's no scope for a horse in either operation. But where foresters are thinning a crop of trees, a horse can be very useful. Cumbersome extraction machines might damage the remaining trees as they remove the surplus logs, whereas a horse can pick its way between them as it takes out the thinnings.

Horses are also valued by forestry contractors in woods which have no access roads or are on steep-sided hillsides. They can pull out trees from areas where tractors can't go – exactly the situation that exists at Sillywrea.

Hauling timber with a single horse in chains is a skilled job. Holding the reins while attaching the unwieldy chain to a log is difficult. And then there's the choice of horse. David has chosen Davey for the job but he's fitted blinkers to him, because the horse might be disconcerted by the sensation of hauling something as unpredictable as a heavy log. On uneven ground a log can bounce and roll. Worse, it can snag on a tree stump and break the chain. Or, in a severe case, hurt the horse.

'You have to be careful,' David says. 'It's a job we like to do with a young-ish horse. Not a young horse, mind, because it's not mature enough. But for a young-ish horse it's good experience working under trees.'

As he hauls the last log away from the wood and over the fields to the farm you can tell Davey is looking forward to getting his nose in his manger. He's sweating from his exertions on a muggy autumn morning.

Auction Marts

John Dodd has been a lifelong supporter of auction marts. He feels they provide a system of buying and selling which has stood the test of time. After all, what could be simpler? The farmer prepares his animals for sale, aiming to show them in the best possible light. They're available for inspection in a pen as they wait to be sold, before being paraded round a ring where potential viewers can see them from all sides. An auctioneer invites the assembled crowd to bid for the animals and they're sold to the person who offers the most money. 'Willing buyer, willing seller. It's a fair way of fixing what something is worth,' says John. 'We've always sold our cattle and sheep that way.'

When there are grumbles from other farmers that butchers are getting too much profit, as there frequently are, John likes to quote the pre-war agricultural writer A.G. Street. 'He was right when he used to say: "Render unto Caesar the things that are Caesar's." If the butchers are making a good profit it will rub off onto the farmers. The farmers' job is to look after the land and produce. Nobody can do everything well. Let the butchers sell the meat, the greengrocers sell the vegetables, the coal merchants the coal. The farmers' place is to produce. If you try and do too many things, you do none of them well.'

Until the middle of the 18th century, farm animals were either reared for the farmer's own use or sold to be consumed in the local village. With the growth of the population of large towns and cities came an increased demand for meat. Drovers with packs of dogs herded groups of cattle long distances to urban markets like Smithfield in London, even going so far as nailing shoes to the beasts' hooves to make sure they lasted the journey. By the middle of the 19th century cattle, sheep, pigs, horses and poultry were being sold in large numbers at 'fairs' in most market towns. Always held on the same day of the week they were chaotic, noisy, foul-smelling gatherings where tethered animals choked the rutted streets, competing for buyers' attentions with farmers' wives proffering eggs, butter and honey, and travellers hawking their wares. Prices were agreed after a great deal of haggling, and the deal sealed by the slap of palms.

Gradually civic pride began to clash with commerce. Pressure grew for the introduction of properly regulated markets which didn't leave streets and pavements awash with animal excrement. Farmers formed themselves into commercial groups and began to raise capital to build marts in the middle of towns close to the agricultural merchants' stores, the banks and, of course, the alehouses. In many cases they were also near a railway station, because as the country opened up with a new network of lines through rural areas, more and more animals were moved by rail.

The usual layout of a mart was a network of holding pens connected to a railed corridor which funnelled sheep, pigs and cattle into the ring where selling took place. In less than a minute the animals were on their way back to the pens, sold to the highest bidder. Initially auction rings were rudimentary places open to the elements, but in time they were covered over and tiered seating was built to form a modern amphitheatre. With some minor adjustments, this is the model that has continued to this day, and when a new mart at Hexham, John's local town, was erected not long ago it was constructed along just such a design.

Hexham is an attractive town whose most famous feature is its abbey, built by St Wilfred between 675 and 680. It is held by many to be the Heart of all England, because it's half-way between the southern coast of England and the most northern tip of Scotland. The assertion that it lies bang in the centre of the whole country is hotly disputed by at least two other nearby places, Allendale and Haltwhistle, but Hexham calmly answers that it laid first claim to the title.

The town was granted a royal market charter in 1662 and markets have been held in the shadow of the abbey walls since that time. The shambles, where traders still sell their merchandise every Tuesday, were erected by a local landowner in 1766. Close to the market place lies Beaumont Street, where William Cook opened Hexham's first auction mart in 1870, not far from the town's corn exchange (now the Queen's Hall) which was built in 1865. Today Beaumont Street is Hexham's most elegant boulevard with a beautiful park on its western side, and it's difficult to imagine animals milling in it 130 years ago.

In 1885, Cook's mart merged with a business run by two brothers called Iveson, and three years later they moved to a site in Maiden's Walk on the eastern edge of Hexham, where the company remained for more than a century. Finally, on 11 August 1995, came the move to a new £4 million auction mart on a greenfield site on the bank of the Tyne. With three selling rings, 21 loading bays and 500 stock pens able to hold 15,000 sheep or 2500 cattle, the mart is a state-of-the-art complex.

Investment on such a scale is a reflection of the confidence shown by Hexham Auction Mart Company in the future of livestock farming. Yet auction marts have had their critics over the years, especially when it comes to selling fattened animals ready for slaughter. The auction company charges a commission of 3 per cent to cover its costs and make a profit. That might seem a bit steep to some. The alternative is to sell primestock direct to an abattoir and cut out the middle man. Many livestock farmers opt for this 'deadweight' system because it saves paying mart commission charges. They contend that the auction is a lottery, with prices up one day and down the next. But John says there is one convincing argument in favour of the auction ring: 'If you don't like the price you're offered you can always pass the animals out and take them back to the farm,' he says. 'To be sure, you've paid to get them there and you'll have to pay to take them home again, but with any luck the trade will be better on another day.'

Auctioneers invariably stress that there's a strong financial advantage to their system: even though a mart may be waiting for payment from the buyers of animals, sellers get their cheques in the next day's post.

Auction marts, like all aspects of agriculture, have been victims of a wave of rationalisation in John's lifetime. Small companies have been swallowed up by large; marts which only held a handful of sales every year have shut down, and many small towns have lost their marts because the land they stood on was worth more for housing than for trading farm stock. Within a 50-mile radius of Sillywrea the last 30 years have seen the disappearance of marts at Cornhill-on-Tweed, Haltwhistle, Fence-houses, Haswell, Blackhill, Kirkcambeck, Threlkeld, Alston, Gateshead, Newcastle, Morpeth, Gilsland and Belford. Yet auction sales of animals have continued to flourish. Until the early months of 2001, that is. With the outbreak of Foot and Mouth disease a shadow was cast over the whole system of selling animals at public auction.

Just to give an impression of the scale of the auction mart system and the amount of money it turns over, these are some figures from the last quarter of a century. In 1976 the through-put of animals through livestock markets in England and Wales was as follows:

3,432,000 cattle
8,883,000 sheep

2,418,000 pigs
1,236,000 calves

That's a grand total of 15,969,000 animals worth £966,493,000 going under auctioneers' hammers during the year.

The figures for 2000 are similar in total but made up in a different way:

1,844,000 cattle
13,740,000 sheep
492,000 pigs
424,000 calves

A total of 16,500,000 animals worth £1,164,147,000 were sold by marts in 2000.

The figures show that there has been a marked fall in the number of cattle, pigs and calves sold by auction. In contrast, the number of sheep has risen sharply. Turnover has not gone up a great deal over the period in question, suggesting that in relative terms, farmers are getting a lot less for their stock than they were 25 years ago.

With changes to farming being mooted in the wake of Foot and Mouth, many are asking: are auction marts' days numbered? Only time will tell. They have served farmers well over the years, but the risk of disease spreading rapidly is inherent in a system which brings together large numbers of farm animals in one place and then disperses them all over the country.

Some have argued in the past that auction marts tend to favour the larger farmer. But the marts reply that they treat all comers the same way. And they have developed a simple way of ensuring that a sense of fairness reigns over the order of selling. A farmer may – quite justifiably – feel aggrieved if his prize animals are chosen to be the first to go in the ring at the start of a day's sale when some buyers may only just be arriving at the mart. Likewise, having to sell last of all may risk getting very few bids at all, because most buyers will have got what they wanted and will be on their way home. So auction marts run a kind of ballot. They encourage farmers to contact them well in advance with details of what they want to sell. It might be 50 Texel-cross lambs, 5 Limousin heifer calves or a dozen ewes with young lambs at foot. The lots are added to a list in the order they arrive. Several days before the sale the mart prints a catalogue of the farms that are selling animals and how many they are bringing. Then a number is drawn out of a hat. It might be '110. Pasture House – 15 Angus steers'. This means that Lot 110 will be first into the ring, followed by 111, down to the end of the list and then from 1 to 109. It's very different from 'first come first served'. It doesn't matter when the entries were phoned in: you can still appear anywhere in the sale. In farmers' parlance 'a good turn' doesn't just mean a favour for a friend. It can also mean being drawn to sell in the middle of a sale, when the bidding is likely to be at its briskest. Farmers will greet each other when they arrive at a sale with 'Got a good turn?' just as often as they will pass a remark about the weather.

For more than half a century, a sale of Suffolk rams has been held at Hexham mart on the last Thursday of September. These are 'commercial' rams intended for cross-breeding as opposed to pedigree sheep used to produce pure-bred animals. For the last 20 years the sale has also included a show with prizes, which is held before selling begins.

The timing of ram sales is not coincidental. Most are held in September to give rams a couple of weeks to settle in on their new farms before being let loose on the ewes round about 14 October. This is the pattern with lowland flocks. In sheep, there are about six months from conception to birth so the aim is to start lambing in the lowlands around 14 March – late enough, it's hoped, to avoid the worst of the winter weather but in time for lambs to be weaned and able to graze when the spring flush of grass comes in May. As a general rule, on hill and upland farms, rams don't go out until around 14 November, with the result that lambing is delayed until 14 April.

John started breeding Suffolk sheep many years ago when he bought a ewe lamb at a gift sale for Hexham Methodist circuit. To raise money for the church, members of the congregation donate a range of home-produced items, varying from scones to flowers and fresh vegetables – and, on that particular occasion, a sheep. The auctioneer knocked it down to John.

The lamb was mated with a Suffolk tup (ram) and duly produced a pair of lambs, which became the foundation of John's flock. Frances and David work closely with John in the development of the bloodlines and the aim is to have about 20 rams for sale every year.

Many farmers sell their Suffolk male breeding sheep as 'ram lambs' when they are just eight months. Even as young as that, they're old enough to sire sheep. But John prefers the rams he sells to have more maturity. So he uses some as ram lambs on his own sheep in their first autumn, and lends some to neighbours. It means that they are 'shearling' rams, aged about 20 months, when he sells them at Hexham.

Some breeders in John's neighbourhood go further than he does in their efforts to persuade farmers to buy their rams at the sale. Four days before, they hold what's called 'Tup Sunday'. This is a day when potential buyers are invited to the breeder's farm, plied with cups of tea (and in some cases, something a bit stronger) and urged to take a close look at the rams due to be sold at the mart the following Thursday. For regular customers, the outing is worth it on two counts. They see the sheep in their own surroundings – and they get a chance to catch up with old friends.

John doesn't feel it's necessary to go to such lengths to market his sheep. He's been relatively happy with the way they've performed over the years. 'Oh, we've toddled along not too badly,' he says. 'Some years prices are up and we've had a good do. Other years it's hardly worth the bother. But you've got to keep trying.'

In the year when the CBTV film crew making *The Last Horsemen* are recording life at Sillywrea, six Suffolk rams have been earmarked to go to the Hexham sale. It's the usual number. Prices for other sheep from the farm aren't as buoyant as they have been in previous years, so the importance of getting good prices at the ram sale is greater than ever.

Preparing animals for a sale is like primping and preening them for the judging at a local agricultural show. It's an art handed down from one generation of stockmen to the next. Fleeces are combed, brushed and snipped with shears. Faces and legs are washed and dried. The aim is to emphasise the animal's good points and if possible hide its faults. Suffolks are short-woolled, black-faced, hornless sheep which came from crossing Norfolk ewes with Southdown rams. They have been recognised as a pure breed since 1810 and are Britain's most popular crossing sheep. They are hardy, prolific and produce fine carcases and heavy fleeces. 'It takes a good sheep to beat a Suffolk,' says John.

Much of the preparation is done back at the farm by David. He doesn't claim to be an expert, but he can draw on years of watching how it's done by people who are. On the morning of the sale he's up early and is soon busy in the sheep pens, where rams are tied by halters while the finishing touches are applied. The sheep will travel to the mart in a cattle waggon, where a lot of the good work can be undone as the animals bump against each other on the short journey. As soon as they arrive at the mart they're guided by 'wallopers' (or, as they're more correctly known, drovers) to their straw-bedded pen. Hanging on the pen rails is a blackboard with a white piece of paper stapled to it. On it is scrawled: Sillywrea. Lot 51.

It's a number they've been dreading, because when the ballot was drawn the number picked out of a hat was 52. It means that John and David's sheep will be the last of all to go through the ring.

John shrugs his shoulders. He says good-naturedly: 'It's still the fairest way to hold a ballot. It has to happen once in a lifetime that you're last. Some years you can benefit from having a late turn because if it's a good trade and prices are better than usual, people hang back hoping to get a bargain at the end of the sale and they get panicky. But I fear that won't happen this year. There are plenty of tups to pick from and I'm afraid the buyers will be finished by the time we start to sell. But that's the luck of farming. There's always another year.'

David and John set to work cleaning and brushing their animals. Faces and heads are vigorously rubbed with a cloth soaked in liquid paraffin to give them an extra shine. The sheep have the numbers 1 to 6 stamped on their backs in red dye. This signifies the order in which they will be sold. It's the result of a lengthy discussion between the two men. Tradition in ram-breeding circles dictates that the best animals should be given odd numbers. It's supposed to send a signal to knowledgeable buyers, alerting them to those animals' superior qualities. However, as in a cricket team, you don't necessarily have your best player opening the batting. It's advisable, the old sheep breeders say, to set a standard by presenting a good sheep to start with and then having your best ram at three or five.

Then again, there can be an element of bluff. You can begin with what you might consider to be a couple of moderate sheep and hope the buyers will pay over the odds for them as they're waiting for the best ones.

Whatever the theory of running orders, John has decided on this occasion to put his best ram into the ring first. He's going to set his stall out from the start. His top rams are 1, 3 and 5. He's hoping they'll do well, at least. 'You can think about it all day but often it doesn't matter how you mark them. Folks just buy what they fancy. It's not what we think they are, it's what others see in them. So, we'll just have to wait and see. We have regular buyers who come back year after year and we hope they'll hang on to the end.'

Each ram is given another number on a tag which has to be tied round the animal's neck on a piece of string. This is its number in the sale, allowing the mart staff to record what it makes when the time comes for it to be sold.

The sale begins at eleven o'clock and the auctioneer sets off at a furious pace. The rams are sold singly and there are 369 to get through. They're selling at a rate of about one a minute, so it will be at least five o'clock before the Sillywrea consignment go under the hammer. David decides to go home to catch up on some unfinished jobs. John heads for the mart cafe for some lunch. This is the social hub of the place, where farmers, dealers and agricultural tradesmen meet for a chat. Prices, trends, the comings and goings on farms in the district, family news. It's all part of the gossip that lubricates the life of the farming community. In the background, there's the relentless drone of the auctioneer working his way through the sheep. Most of them seem to be making about £200.

At quarter to five, the moment has come. John follows his rams through a series of pens until they arrive at the edge of the ring. He's still patting and brushing them, almost as a nervous reaction, hoping that one last stroke will make them look even better. 'Flat back, good hips, tight skin,' he says. 'That's what the buyers are looking for.'

Most of the seats overlooking the ring were full when the sale was at its height but they're empty now and only a handful of farmers are left. Nevertheless, there's an old adage that 'a man who bids is worth a lot of lookers-on'. The hope is that the remaining few will like what they see and vie furiously with one another.

Number one trots into the ring, with John not far behind. There isn't much time to tell the auctioneer about the ram in front of him. 'Used as a lamb,' John says, indicating that the shearling has already spent one autumn as a sire. This may sound strange to an outsider, but it is a coded way of saying the ram can breed. Buyers won't be getting an infer-

tile tup. The auctioneer repeats the information in a mechanical way but seems eager to
get finished. After all, it's the end of a long
day. 'Lot 51,' he intones. 'Sillywrea.' And
immediately the bidding begins. A mart lad
taps the ram as it circles the sawdust-strewn
arena. John waves his brush at the animal. It's
important to keep it moving, both to display
its good points and, hopefully, to hide any
weaknesses it might have. The bidding
reaches £280 before the ram is knocked
down to one of John's regular buyers.

One by one the rams charge into the ring.
The auctioneer works hard to get a good
price for all of them. There's more interest
in some than others, but it's difficult to see
why Number 3, despite its key spot in the
running order, only makes £120 but
number 5 quickly goes up to £280. After all
six have been sold John is £1,000 better off.

The auctioneer's assistant, who makes a
note of who's bought what, tears off a sheet
with the details and gives it to John. He scans
it, noting that two of the rams were bought
by regular buyers. One had stuck it out to the
last after all. Another had gone home and
returned to the mart to bid for John's sheep.
'That's loyalty for you,' John grins.

A Welsh farmer who bought a sheep sidles

up to John. 'Any luck?' he asks. It's a question which would mystify anyone not acquainted with the ancient traditions of farmers' marts. It refers to the custom whereby the seller gives the buyer a 'luck penny' to wish him luck with the animal he's bought. These days, however, it's more like a 'luck pound'. For years there have been attempts to have this custom outlawed, but to no avail. It's endemic in the livestock industry where buying and selling is part of life. Perhaps there's a feeling that you'll be paying it one day, but getting it back the next. As it happens, John's come prepared. He slips the man a couple of coins.

'Will you "stand behind" your rams?' another buyer asks, meaning: are they guaranteed 'stock-getters'? In other words, are they fertile?

John replies: 'They're natural reared, not forced. And they've been used as lambs. You'll not have any bother with them.'

At his pen, John's joined by David, who's hurried back to the mart in the hope of seeing the rams being sold. Frances had rung the auction company to see what stage the sale was at. 'They were selling Lot 47 so I thought I might get there in time,' he says. 'In the event, I just missed them.' He and his father-in-law look at their rams for the last time. In a couple of hours, the sheep will be on their way to pastures new. 'Aye,' John says. 'A thousand pounds for six sheep. Nothing to go into raptures about but not too bad in the circumstances. Maybe there were a couple which were too little money and I should have passed them out of the ring, but on the whole it wasn't the disaster it might have been, given the fact that we were last in the sale. In farming you've just got to keep going and hope for a better day next time.'

The Auctioneer

One farming character that John has known for many years is Maurice Reed, a director of Hexham Auction Mart Company, breeder of Suffolk sheep and an auctioneer whose prominent part in the local farming scene was recognised when he was awarded the MBE in 1998. Maurice, a farmer's son from the remote village of Sparty Lea, high on the Pennines in south-west North-umberland, has been involved in the auction trade for nearly 50 years.

He loves to expound on the art of auction-eering: 'You've got to have a presence. I insist on standing when I'm selling. I've always believed you're not doing your job properly if you're sat in a chair. You must make your presence felt.

'You've got to have a good knowledge, firstly of what you are selling but also who's buying. You've got to know the class of stock they particularly like. There are certain buyers round a ring, when an animal comes in, you don't even need to look at them. You know they'll be interested. You must do a lot of research, particularly on your seasonal sales. Look through the catalogues for the previous two years and make a note of the prices a farmer's animals made last year and who bought them. It gives you a starting point.'

Maurice has sold non-stop for hours at some of the company's largest sheep sales. 'I once sold 13,000 lambs in a day and never left the auctioneer's box from half past ten in the morning to six in the evening. You don't eat – you haven't time. You just snatch cups of tea and sweat so much you don't need to go to the toilet. I'm not sure it's the best way. I've had two hips replaced and it's probably because of all those hours on my feet in the rostrum.

'The main part of selling is knowing where to start an animal. You can't wait for bids otherwise you'd be on all day. Once you've got a sale going you've got to run up bids to where you feel they should be. The best lambs may be making £70, so you'll start them at £55. You don't get much of a chance to see the stock, so it's your first impression as they walk through the gate into the ring. You have to make an instant decision what you think they might be worth and then work hard to get it. The way animals are presented is crucial. Really skilled stockmen can transform the way their cattle and sheep look by washing them and clipping their coats.

'The mart system brings the best out of farmers. They know if they want to shine they have to manage their stock properly, dress them properly and present them properly in the ring. It keeps them on their toes. As well as that, they want to beat their neighbours. It's a competitive streak. They hope their neighbours will be talking about their stock when they're out for a drink at night. If marts disappeared, the quality of stock would fall. Farmers' pride in their stock would vanish.'

Maintaining the momentum of a sale can be difficult. 'The better the trade, the longer it takes to sell something,' Maurice says. 'I know that sounds a bit odd. But what happens is you have more bidders and you've got to keep looking round a packed ring making sure you don't miss anyone. With the opposite situation, when the trade is dragging a bit and you haven't as many bidders, you can often sell faster.'

Over the years Maurice has built up a collection of auctioneer's hammers and chairman's mallets. 'One farmer who was retiring, we were handling his sale, he made me a nice rosewood hammer with an ivory tip. And another one that was made for me is a red walnut gavel which you hold between your fingers and bring down like a stamp when you've sold something.'

Maurice likes to introduce a note of drama into farm property sales – where the house, buildings and land are up for auction. Invariably, large sums of money are at stake and buyers tend to hold back. To concentrate their minds, Maurice is apt to produce an hour-glass containing 20 seconds of sand. As the sand runs out, he likes to warn the audience in deeply serious tones that the property is going ... going ... gone. It usually has the desired effect.

Religion

There's a fine crop of swedes in Lanefoot Field, and David and John are bent over the rows, ripping up the biggest ones and paring off the roots with their pocket knives. They fill a sack with the bulky cream-and-purple swedes, before switching their attentions to another crop nearby. A graipe (fork) is thrust under the row and a handful of white 'taties' (potatoes) emerges from the sandy soil. The two men pick a few pounds before making their unhurried way back to the farm, each with a sack over his shoulder.

It's a ritual which is repeated every year at the end of September. The horsemen are collecting produce from the land to take to the harvest festival at their local Methodist church. 'All the farmers round about give something,' John says. 'It's a tradition that goes back a long time.'

A long time to be sure. In fact, there's been a strong Methodist tradition in the area round Sillywrea for more than two and a half centuries. The Wesleyan chapel at

Hindley Hill in the hamlet of Keenley, just a mile and a half away as the crow flies, is the oldest in the north of England.

Students of religion will know that the driving forces behind the Methodist movement were John Wesley and his brother Charles. In 1729, while they were still undergraduates at Oxford, they formed a religious society which promoted piety and morality in a reaction against the perceived apathy of the Church of England at that time. They were called Methodists because of 'the regularity of their lives as well as their studies'. When they left university they made it their task to spread their version of the Gospel. During his lifetime John Wesley gave 40,000 sermons and rode thousands of miles on horseback to preach in remote areas.

It was in July 1747 that the process of conversion to Methodism began in Allendale, a small town which lies three miles south of Sillywrea. A contemporary account describes it like this: 'One summer's day the peaceful inhabitants were startled by a crowd gathering round the market cross. There stood a tall, stalwart young man, not more than 25 years of age, with uncovered head and a book in his hand. His face was open and honest and he spoke to them with an earnest and ready eloquence. Scriptures seemed to be at his fingers' ends and his powerful voice made such an echo in their astonished hearts that they urged him to visit them again.'

The preacher was a disciple of John Wesley. His name was Christopher Hopper.

One of the people listening from the edge of the crowd was a young man with a fighting cock slung in a sack over his shoulder. Jacob Rowell had spent much of his young life gambling and drinking, but on hearing Hopper he vowed to give up his vices and become a Methodist. 'The word reached his heart and thus was this blasphemer and injurious person brought to the feet of Jesus.'

Rowell's own power of oratory became legendary. 'His preaching was accompanied with such power that some who could not see him for the crowds who gathered in the doorway of the house were prostrated by the word.'

This was so common that Rowell acquired the name 'Fell-'em-i'-th'-heck', meaning 'He knocks them down at the door'. For 40 years the former cock-fighter went forth to deliver his message 'amid untold perils on snowy mountain roads and among violent men – often preaching with the blood running down his face. Richly did he deserve the epitaph John Wesley gave him of a "faithful old soldier".'

Christopher Hopper and Jacob Rowell had prepared the way for John Wesley to visit Allendale, and in August 1748 the evangelist went there with his friends, having stayed overnight with them at Hindley Hill. It was a Friday, the day of the weekly market, and as well as some of the local farmers and their wives the town was full of miners who had come to collect their half-year pay from the local lead mining company offices.

'As well as this unusual congregation of dalesmen and daleswomen the Church of England clergyman had also beat up a little army of opponents and was eager to dispute every word,' the contemporary account relates. 'But Mr Wesley allowed him to run off his lesson and calmly turned to his work.'

From these beginnings Methodism spread through the isolated parishes that lie on both sides of the northern Pennines. Wesley and his brother moved on, leaving preachers like Hopper and Rowell to consolidate their work. The simplicity of their message appealed to the dales people and they threw themselves into raising money for their new faith. After the first chapel was built at

Keenley in 1750, chapels sprang up in many dales villages over the next century. And as the years went by Sunday schoolrooms were built on to them where for the first time many children received some basic teaching.

A short history of Methodism in Allendale, printed in 1890, remarks: 'Such are the fruits of Methodism in a secluded and little-known part of our country. It has sought the elevation of a comparatively neglected population and it has not laboured in vain. Hundreds of children have received in its Sunday schools their only education and an army of Christian labourers has been raised to ennobling service as lay preachers, class leaders and school teachers, who, but for its presence and influence, would have had neither motive nor opportunity for self-improvement.'

Side by side with the introduction of Methodism was the spread of the Temperance movement. The British and Foreign Temperance Society was founded in 1831 and the London Temperance League in 1851. Their message of moderation in all things – and abstinence from alcohol – found a welcoming audience in those north of England districts that had embraced the Methodist message. A Temperance Society established at Langley, John Dodd's local village, was well supported. A poster dated 1862 advertised the society's annual picnic, to be held in a field at Staward Pele. According to the local paper, the Langley Mill Band opened the proceedings at noon, playing a slow march from *Lucia di Lammermoor*, followed by a series of addresses, musical items and cups of tea. The day closed with the playing of the National Anthem as the sun was setting. 'It ended well before I was born, but from what I've heard it was a tremendous affair with crowds of people coming up on the train to hear the Temperance speakers,' says John. 'My grandfather was prominent in the Temperance Society. He was one of the organisers of the picnic and it was his horses which used to lead the tables out to the field.

'The Methodists used to be very strict on the drink. Many still won't touch a drop. For myself, I might have a shandy, very occasionally. But that's strong enough for me.'

A new religion can split communities, however, just as it can unite them. And Langley was the scene of just such a falling-out. In the 1840s two Methodist sects flourished in the Langley area. They were the Wesleyan Methodists – founded, as the name implies, by John Wesley – and the Primitive Methodists – formed in the early 19th century by men who believed that the established Methodist church had become 'too respectable' and no longer appealed to the working class and the poor. Subsistence farming, coal mining and lead smelting were the main industries throughout the north Pennines at that time, and the Primitives attracted a large following among families working in them.

In 1849 the Wesleyan Methodists leased some land from the Lord Commissioners of the Greenwich Hospital for five shillings a year and proceeded to build a chapel. They had previously been sharing a 'preaching room' in the village with the Primitive Methodists, so they agreed to allow the Primitives to use the new chapel for their meetings.

For some reason which has not been recorded, there was friction between the two sects. It came to a head when one of them prevented the other from holding their usual Sunday service in the chapel by using the simple expedient of ... talking. And talking. And talking.

In the time-honoured practice of MPs who want to block the progress of a Bill through Parliament, they simply talked their opponents out!

History doesn't record who was at fault. But the reaction of the Langley Primitive Methodists was to seek a new home. They met in members' houses for a few years and held fundraising evenings. At last, in 1870, they themselves applied to Greenwich Hospital, to lease some land at Deanraw Quarter, and there they built a new chapel.

Ironically, the older chapel eventually ceased to be used for worship – it is now the village hall – whereas the 'new' chapel continues to hold services to this day, albeit attended by a fraction of the congregation that once filled its pews.

In the mid-1880s John's Methodist ancestors showed their independence of spirit once again when they and other members of the congregation decided it would be a good idea to build a caretaker's house for the new chapel. Permission had to be sought from Methodist Church authorities in London.

John tells what happened next. 'For some reason best known to themselves, "Headquarters" didn't agree with us building a cottage for the caretaker. They didn't go along with the idea of a tied house. But that didn't stop my fore elders. Where the chapel's situated it needs a caretaker. Just a part-time job, that's all. So several members of the congregation, my grandfather among them, just went ahead regardless of what they'd been told to do. They went off to the quarry and led stone with their carts and horses and built the cottage anyway.'

John grins wickedly. The mental picture of independent northerners cocking a snook at stuffy Londoners appeals greatly to him. 'I've told some of the Methodist ministers since, when they try to enforce the laws of Headquarters, that we're pretty near to the Border here at Langley. We're stubborn Borderers and, you know, we don't always do as we're told.'

In 1903, a schoolroom was added to the chapel so that Sunday school lessons could be held there. They lasted until 1967 when the teacher retired and no one came forward to take her place.

The Dodd family has been one of the mainstays of the chapel. An article in the *Hexham Courant* dated 26 May 1888 describes a 'public tea' held by the Primitive Methodists at Langley to celebrate the anniversary of their Sabbath school. Among the people presiding over the tables were the Misses Dickinson, John's ancestors. Today

Frances is treasurer and John is steward. Maggie, who was secretary for years, says: 'It's always been part of our life.'

John may be a strong Methodist but he doesn't discount other religions: 'My own feelings are: it doesn't matter what Christian faith you're in, we're all brothers. We've always been a Methodist family, but I think it's just the family you're born into. We're all different. What I believe as a religion wouldn't necessarily suit the modern-day believers. At the same time what I believe wouldn't have suited generations before me either. The way I see it is this: there's bound to be a plan somewhere or other; things just don't happen willy nilly. We're here to prove our worth, that's the way I look at it; we're here to prove our worth.'

David has a similar view. 'I would describe myself first as a Christian, then as a Methodist, because all the churches are very similar. I was brought up in a Congregational church and then I went to a Church of England church. Now we attend the Methodist church.

'I don't get to chapel as often as I would like, but outside of chapel, yes, Christianity does play a part in my life. I feel that you need to believe in something and I think that subconsciously what you believe in shapes the way you are.'

Darkness is falling outside the church as people begin to arrive for the harvest festival and evening of entertainment. Among the farmers are some familiar faces: John's life-long friend, timber merchant Martin Jackson and his wife Winnie, and the local auctioneer, Maurice Reed with his wife Susan.

The organ strikes up with the chords for 'Praise Oh Praise Our God and King' and the congregation joins in with gusto. At the end of the hymn everyone kneels. The lay preacher begins: 'For the harvest of the autumn, for the fertility of the land and for Your bounty of sustained providence we give thanks. We enjoy all these untold blessings.'

Every corner of the chapel is decorated with bunches of flowers. At one side, set against the pine panelling, is a vast table covered with a white cloth on which is arranged a mountain of home-made pro-duce: gingerbread, scones, cakes, jams, mar-malade, chutney, pickled onions and pickled cabbage. Mingled with this are huge leeks, baskets of potatoes, and rows of washed swedes from Sillywrea. Bowls of grapes and other fruit lend added colour to the display.

The lay preacher's address is followed by a

concert: a guitar and keyboard duo singing a selection of religious Country and Western songs like 'The Old Country Church' and 'The Wonder of It All'. Then comes the highlight of the evening: the auction of all the produce.

David and John hold aloft onions, bunches of flowers, cabbages, Maggie's jars of pickled onions and marmalade – and the potatoes and swedes they picked earlier in the day. Local auctioneer Brian Rogerson conducts the sale, putting as much effort into it as he would when selling a pen of sheep. Bidding is animated – it's the kind of activity that comes naturally to a farming community. But people are generous too: a home-baked fruit cake sells for £8.50.

'The produce is typical of the rural church. It's certain to be home produced, home cooked,' says the local Methodist minister, the Rev. David Perkins, who is in the congregation. 'You go to a town church and it's more likely to be packets and tins: sardines and baked beans. The rural church, it's an offering of people's talents and gifts. They grow up with the food, as it were, and bring it to the church. They celebrate the creativity of God in a simple way.'

In the Sunday school room a fire is blazing.

Water is heated, tea is brewed and the final part of the evening gets under way: a chance to chat over a plateful of sandwiches and cake. People who have bought produce in the sale line up to pay Frances. It all goes towards helping the church to survive.

Langley Methodist Church is well supported in the sense that people turn up in healthy numbers for special events like the harvest festival (last weekend in September), the chapel anniversary (first Sunday in July), a bring-and-buy sale (beginning of June) and Silver Tree (second week in December). The visitors are mostly Methodists from other villages in the area. It's part of their tradition to go round as many churches as possible to help them celebrate similar dates on their calendars. They're social occasions as well as religious gatherings.

'It's really an occasion for the smaller churches to support one another,' says David Perkins. 'People feel a great commitment to each other's churches and they will go to a number of different harvest festivals to demonstrate their friendship. The cycle of events will be held every year at small rural churches throughout this valley.'

In terms of weekly services, however, attendances are small. Sometimes only half a dozen worshippers make their way to the church on a Sunday evening, and half of them come from John's family.

'Langley is by and large a farming community and this is a church which has been kept going by farming families and country people,' says the minister. 'There's always a nagging fear that the Methodist movement may die out in sparsely populated rural areas. But people have been saying that for 60 years and while some churches have closed, most still manage to keep going.

'It's true younger families coming with their children are getting thinner on the ground, mainly because the number of people who work on the farms has fallen so dramatically But the people are still there so maybe the Church has to change to appeal to them.'

Horse Sale

On a table in the parlour of William Wordsworth's house at Cockermouth in Cumbria is a faded copy of the *Cumbrian Packet* dated Tuesday, 22 April 1777. The newspaper is one of the many historical artefacts displayed in the rooms of the Georgian town house where the poet was born in 1770. As was the custom in those days, the broadsheet's front page consists of column after column of adverts and announcements. Among them, a small paragraph proclaims that horse sales 'will be held at Market Hill in the town of Wigton in Cumberland on 20th February and 25th September 1778 and will continue annually on the same two days in future'. The notice adds: 'The fairs are well known to be as good as any in the country' and promises 'a great showing of horses'. Clearly the tradition for horse sales at Wigton was already well established by this stage of the 18th century. It proves that things don't change a lot in the countryside; an event that took place annually more than two and a half centuries ago is still being held today – in the same market town and at more or less the same time of year. Even the currency for trading horses is the same: they're still sold in guineas.

Wigton Horse Sale takes place on the last Wednesday of October. John has been a regular visitor since he was a boy and in nearly 60 years he's only missed it once.

These days the sale is organised by Hope's Auction Company a firm which was founded in 1890 and which has witnessed the rise and fall of the heavy horse at close quarters.

At its peak in the 1930s, Wigton was the largest sale of horses in the country with a catalogued entry every year of between 1000 to 1500. So many animals were on offer that the sale lasted three days. Heavy work horses the first day, unbroken work horses the second and riding horses the third. Most of the work horses were Clydesdales. Cumberland studs were famous countrywide for the Clydesdale stock they produced, and buyers would come from as far afield as Aberdeen and Southampton. Pubs were overflowing with customers, stables were brimming with horses, saddlers were hard at work selling their bridles and harness from stalls all round the market and dealers were busily buying horses by the load for clients like railway companies and breweries. One of their mottos was 'Well bought, half sold', meaning they were half-way towards making a profit on a horse if they didn't pay too much for it in the first place.

Today's Wigton Horse Sale is a far cry from the booming event of yesteryear. It's been reduced to one day and most of the entries are hunters and ponies.

In the year that a CBTV camera crew accompanies John, David, Norman and Richard to the sale only 24 of the 140 entries are Clydesdales. Not that they're going to let that spoil their day out. John says they're here for social as well as business reasons. 'We come to see the horse trade and get an idea of what the horses in the rest of the country are like. We meet a lot of friends and get the crack. It's amazing what tips you can pick up about what's happening in the horse world. It's educational as well as a good day off.'

He's not intending to buy a horse this time, having purchased a foal last year. Five horses of different ages are enough for Sillywrea. In a couple of years' time it may be necessary to bring in a replacement as one of the older horses gets closer to retirement.

The Wigton sale may be a shadow of its former self, but it's still a colourful event buzzing with visitors. Horses are being ridden up and down the alleyways between the pens, people are studying their catalogues, and shrewd judges of horseflesh are leaning over the rails, patting flanks and stroking necks. Old-timers are deep in conversation, earnestly comparing the merits of one breed with another.

'Mind out, Richard, there's a horse coming,' John warns his grandson, as a woman on a huge hunter clatters her way through the mart. 'You've got to have eyes in the back of your head at a sale like this.'

What sort of horses come to Wigton? 'Well,' John says after running his eyes over the various entries, 'the best ones generally get sold privately at home and don't get brought to the market, but there are one or two useful horses here today.'

What are the points to look for in a Clydesdale? 'It's a pretty good saying: "no foot no horse". You want to start and judge from the feet. They must have good, sound feet. Nice flat bone with the hocks turned in, not too long in the back and not too short either, good sprung ribs, nice silky hair.'

After chatting to old friends and catching up on all the gossip, John and his family take up their position at the ringside and wait for the sale to start at 10.30. First into the ring is a placid nine-year-old Shire mare. The auctioneer sets to work, inviting bids. John says to Richard: 'Don't wave your hand. We don't want a horse!'

John and David have a good memory for horses' pedigrees. 'The horses' breeding is listed in the catalogue and over the years you get to know which stallions breeders are using,' John says.

As soon as a horse comes into the ring John's watching to see who's bidding for it. 'I can picture what kind of a life most of them are going to have. Some will be going for show work, some will be going for breeding. I know most of the men who are buying them.'

It goes without saying that none of the Clydesdales are destined for farm work.

Three-quarters of the way through the heavy horses John and David's attention is caught by Garff Satellite, a seven-month-old bay Clydesdale colt foal bred by Sir Charles Kerruish at Maughold on the Isle of Man. It's an exceptional foal, but there doesn't seem to be much interest in it. John's genuinely saddened when it's sold for just 160 guineas. For the breeder, who's paid transport across the Irish Sea, a £15 entry fee and £8 auctioneer's commission, there's not much profit left.

John feels he's missed a bargain, and after the work horses have been sold he goes to look longingly at the foal. 'I'll think about it for a long time. We bought Robin from the same man at 300 guineas – that's my limit

295

for buying a foal – and honestly speaking, today's was better at 160. But that's just the luck of the game. We can't accommodate another horse at the moment. Whenever you really want anything it's always a good price and when you haven't space for something it's cheap.'

John is also enough of a realist to know that falling prices for the horses he loves don't bode well for the future. A breeder might have to pay £150 for a stud fee and then keep a pregnant mare for a year. If all they get for the resultant foal is 160 guineas, why should they bother? 'There was a bit of a revival in heavy horses a few years ago, but when you see so few Clydesdales at a sale like this – and prices so low – you do begin to worry about what might happen in the years to come. It's very depressing. I don't want to start breeding them myself. It's too expensive.'

He has one last ritual to perform before heading home: buying a couple of pounds of Cumberland sausage from Wharton's, the butchers next to the market. 'Can't come to Cumbria and not buy some Cumberland sausage,' he grins. 'I've been doing it for years.'

Winter

Ploughing Lea

The curfew tolls the knell of parting day
The lowing herd wind slowly o'er the lea
The ploughman homeward plods his weary
  way,
And leaves the world to darkness and to
  me.

In 1751, when Gray's *Elegy* immortalised
the 'rude forefathers' of a country hamlet,
half the population of England eked out a
living from the land. Now the number of
people still involved in agriculture is less
than two per cent. But at Sillywrea, there
are still echoes of rural life as it was in the
poet's time. In the chill of a clear December
morning John heads for the Kiln Field with
two of his horses. He's looking forward to
another day spent on one of his great joys:
ploughing lea. Later, like the ploughman in
Gray's poem, he'll make his way homeward
as darkness creeps in and the fields are
bathed in moonlight.

Grassland is either temporary or

permanent. In the former, often called 'temporary ley' or 'lea', seeds of grasses and clovers are sown on a newly ploughed field, and after a period of time the land is ploughed up again. Permanent grassland, on the other hand, remains continuously under grass and is generally called meadow or pasture. It may have been grass from time immemorial, or it may have been created more recently by sowing a mixture of grass seeds containing long-lasting varieties such as timothy and cocksfoot as well as high-yielding rye-grasses.

A brick-making business existed two centuries ago at Sillywrea. Located close to a supply of blue clay, 12 kilns produced bricks for buildings, pantiles for roofs and clay tiles for field drains. A relic of those times remains in the shape of two squat brick kilns at the side of Kiln Field. All around them, the soil is full of shards of brick which rise to the surface every time the field is ploughed.

When pressed, John can close his eyes and imagine the layout of Sillywrea with its ancient field boundaries. 'I know them well, all the fields on the farm,' he says. 'On the Ordnance Survey Map they're all called something different.' The roll-call of field names is like a history of the farm: 'There's the Big Allotment, which we call The Fell; Moss Flats, because it's got a mossy bit in the middle; Shillows, which we call the Quarry Field because that's where they quarried the stone to build the new farmhouse in 1870; The Thackie, because there used to be an old thatched cottage in the corner; Bob's Field, because it once belonged to a chap called Bob Hutchison; The Cow Pasture, next to the house; Barley Rigg, House Field, Corner Field, Front Field, First Low Field, Second Low Field, Hawthorns, Wheat Hill, Sheep Hills. In my life I've cut all but one of them for hay, and I've ploughed all except four.'

John explains why he's decided to plough out the Kiln Field. 'This field's been down to grass for 15 years, which is maybe a bit too long. Ploughing it buries the docks and nettles as well as turning over the grass. It'll benefit in a number of ways.

'Ploughing lea, someone once wrote, is the pleasantest disguise manual work can take. I wouldn't disagree with them. It's a lovely job, just up and down, nice and steady. Trying to make a good job. If a ploughman has two good horses he's halfway there. These two, Davey and Sandy, they work well together. For a young horse, Sandy's exceptional. He's as steady as a rock. He's walking in the furrow, which I used to be told was harder than walking on the land. But he's stepping away as easy as can be.'

Bathed in a yellow mid-winter light, ploughman and team work calmly up and down the field, turning at the end of each row with John patiently urging: 'Come in lads, get on bonny lads, get on.'

Farm Sale

It was the wettest day of the winter. On fields planted with winter barley wheat the water ran in rivulets down the rows, washing away copious amounts of soil. Roads were flooded, walls collapsed, trees were toppled, rivers burst their banks and homes were threatened. Sensible people battened down the hatches. They threw another bucket of coal on the fire or turned up the central heating and sat tight while the rain lashed the countryside.

For John and David, however, Saturday 25 October was a day they'd been looking forward to, and they weren't going to let a spot of bad weather spoil their plans. There was a retirement sale at Sharpley Farm at Humshaugh near Hexham. They were going to go, come hell or high water.

Sharpley lies north of the Roman Wall, in an area which is well off the beaten track, but people seem to be having no trouble finding it. Cars, pickups, jeeps pulling trailers and Land Rovers with horseboxes are strung out along the narrow road past the farm, none daring to park in a field in case they sink in. John has been joined by Norman Barber, and David has his son Richard with him. They head straight for the field where the farm tools and implements are laid out in the teeming rain. All four are wearing their best waterproofs and Wellingtons. But by the time they've reached the first lot, they are soaked.

John, however, seems not to notice. As a prospector in a gold rush might dig for nuggets, so John is searching for items which are of particular value to him. Cold and wet he may be, but he is warmed on the inside by a spark of delicious anticipation. Perhaps the people he normally competes with for 'bygones' – the townies, the antique dealers and the collectors – will be put off by the rain.

The men who traditionally ran small mixed farms like Sharpley couldn't afford to pay people to do many of the routine jobs, so they became all-rounders, turning their hands to anything. The collection of objects now being examined by John and Norman reflects that. There is a set of mole-traps, proof that the farmer preferred to carry out his own vermin control rather than summon the local mole-catcher. Wire-stretchers and a hefty post hammer are evidence that he fixed his own boundaries without the help of a fencing contractor. Draining rods, sweeps' brushes, a saw bench, a portable blacksmith's forge: all are signs that here was a Jack of all trades – and master of most too, it seems.

Auctioneers like Trevor Simpson have to work hard when they're selling in a deluge. A joke here, a bit of banter there keeps the sale alive. 'I can't see you bidding, Dave,' he says to a man with his brim pulled down against the rain. 'Tip your hat back a bit!' He must move rapidly from lot to lot, chivvying buyers and creating a momentum so that prices don't drift downwards. Newspaper reporters were always taught to carry a pencil so that they could keep making notes in the rain. It's the same rule for auctioneers and their assistants, who have to keep note of what's being sold.

Underfoot, the field where the sale is being held is turning into a quagmire. The crowd squelches from one lot to another, drawn onwards by a curiosity which only public auction can satisfy: what is that thing worth? In the case of a collection of old bridles, leather straps and horse breeching, not much, John is hoping. The auctioneer starts them off at £5, the rhythm of his delivery inviting higher bids: 'Five, five, five, five, five pound bid, five pound bid, five pound bid, six, six, six, six pound bid, six pound bid, seven, seven pound, seven pound I'm bid, seven pound I'm bid, seven pounds, seven pounds, seven pounds, Dodd, Sillywrea.' John's face has barely moved a muscle during the bidding. Years of standing at auctions have taught him it's better to remain as anonymous as possible in the hope that no new buyer will jump in. He uses the same time-honoured tactics when the next lot comes up. For £17, he snaps up two sodden horse collars but decides not to go after another pile of rusty bridles, even though they only make £4.

In a pool of water an old Ransome horse plough waits to be sold. In the 1950s and

1960s these ancient machines turned up at sales in their thousands, unwanted reminders of a pre-mechanised age. One or two were bought at knockdown prices by men like John. But most went for scrap. In the last 20 years the picture has changed. First a wave of nostalgia for a lost age brought people to farm sales looking for ploughs they could display outside pubs or on their own front lawns. Then came the collectors. Sometimes they were men who had retired from farming but who wanted to retain a connection with their past. Other times they were people who had no links with the land but were just fascinated by country lore or forgotten rustic skills. Whatever the cause, the price of iron horse ploughs is higher than it's been for years.

To counter this trend, John tries a familiar tactic: start the bidding off as low as possible. The auctioneer, as ever, is optimistic. 'Now the plough. Where shall I start? Fifty, twenty, a tenner?' Silence. 'Five pounds then. Five pounds?' Silence. 'Two,' says John. The auctioneer: 'Two pound I'm bid. Two pound. Two pound.' But the ploy doesn't really work. Bidding is brisk. John drops out at £85 and the plough is sold for £90 to the man from Beamish Museum.

John's mildly disappointed. 'It's a good plough, with a grand mouldboard,' he says to David. 'But I knew he would keep bidding so I had to pull out. Anyway, we have plenty of ploughs at home.'

The rain's beginning to take its toll. The crowd's thinning out. The men from Sillywrea are soaked to the skin but they have no intention of leaving. That bargain could be just round the corner. John pays £85 for a set of chain harrows, which he considers good value. Next comes a set of metal zigzag cornharrows. There are no takers at all for them and John gets them for £1. He can hardly conceal his delight. 'They're bound to be a lucky packet,' he smiles.

As the sale draws to an end, the rain ceases and the sun shines weakly across the saturated landscape. A rainbow appears in the east. John shakes the water from his cap and pronounces himself satisfied with his day. 'I feel sorry for the man who's selling,' he says. 'It's the end of a lifetime in farming for him. But a sale's never the same if it's put off. They were right to press ahead, and he seems to have got some good prices.

'We've got some useful things. The horse collars are a bit small for work horses but they will come in handy for a young horse when we're breaking it in. And the other stuff was cheap, so I'm pleased.'

John, David and Richard make their way back to the farm through a countryside sodden with rain. Near Haydon Bridge the road is under two feet of water. They turn round and take another road. John recalls a previous time when he was out with Maggie at night and they came across the same spot. 'I just drove into it,' he recalls. 'The next thing I knew, the car was full of water and Maggie's umbrella was swimming round the back seat like a fish.'

At Sillywrea, a vast spread awaits the men: scones, muffins, lemon cake, fruit cake, iced sponge cake, bread, cheese, jam, apple pie and teacake. Scalding hot tea by the mugful. John recounts what he's bought at the sale, just as he must have done countless times before. Maggie and Frances listen, amused. They love to hear who was at the sale, and who bought what.

'David got some swingletrees and I got some little things off the trailer, augers and such like,' John says. 'However, anything I wanted, as soon as I started bidding, someone else seemed to want it too. But the chain harrows, I was determined I would make somebody pay for them. Our own are done and these would be £400 new. But I got them for £85. And then I got some zigzag harrows for a pound. They were cheap. Mind, it's a true saying: nothing's cheap unless you have a use for it.'

His wife says drily: 'Did you get a new catch for the yard gate?' It's a standing joke in the family that small everyday repairs often go unheeded while there's horse work to do.

Unconcerned by Maggie's gentle teasing, her husband goes on to list his other purchases, including a small weighing machine for £5. 'Oh,' he adds, remembering his other coup, 'we got some harness too.' Frances says, with just a touch of irony: 'Surprise, surprise!' She's seen many a day when her father has returned from a farm sale with some old harness. 'Ah,' says John, smiling. 'This was different. It was britching harness. Just what we need at the moment!'

Mucking Out

Farmyard manure is distinguished by the fact that it contains all the constituents which the land requires in order to grow good crops.

Fream's Elements of Agriculture, 1895

The cycle of farming is an unending one. Sowing, harvesting, storing, winter feeding. Just as the farmer spends all summer gathering together feed for winter, so his winter is spent distributing that feed and cleaning up the results after the cattle have eaten it. And just as the land provides that feed, so it too has to be fed.

Today's farms have sophisticated systems for storing and disposing of manure: on dairy farms tractor-mounted scrapers push it into holding tanks from which it's pumped into spreaders and sprayed on the fields. On beef farms it's grabbed in huge bites by mechanical grabs and dumped into tractor-driven muckspreaders. Rarely does anyone pick up a shovel or a fork.

But at Sillywrea, mucking out is a daily manual job carried out the same way as it has been for more than a century. Cows are tied up in a series of small byres and the only way to remove the manure and soiled bedding straw is by brush and shovel. Being an old farm steading, the byres are grouped closely together and access for modern machinery would be difficult. But one of the advantages of having horses is that a cart can be backed up close to the byre door to receive the shovelfuls of muck. 'The way the farm's laid out this suits our system,' John says. 'It's hard work, make no mistake about it. But I've never minded hard work. Before David, when there was only me, I used to get up at half past four in the morning and have all the byres mucked out by breakfast at eight o'clock. That's two cartloads. No wonder I had a heart attack!'

The muck is led out by horse and cart to the fields. The hinged endboard is removed from the cart and a 'muck hack' (long-handled muck fork) used to drag it off the cart and dump it in small heaps, five yards apart, with five yards between the rows. This is a pattern John learned from his father, who in turn learned it from his father. But today, this is a unique scene. It's almost certain that no other working farm in the country is still handling its muck in this way.

Seen from afar, the fields appear pockmarked with neat rows of black dots. It's only in the spring, when John and David return to those fields with graipes to spread the muck by hand, that the reason for dropping them in regular heaps is clear: it ensures an even coverage of the field.

'I don't know what other people do – well, there won't be many handling muck in the old-fashioned way like we do – but I reckon I can spread 40 heaps in an hour. In fact, you could almost set your watch by it,' says John.

Spreading muck brings back memories of Irish workers who used to call at the farm to see if there was any casual work. 'They were fantastic workers,' John recalls. 'Using a graipe, shovel or hoe they had few equals. I remember once – and it shows how times have changed – one of these chaps came into a field like this and said, "I'll spread the whole lot for £20," and he did it in four days. In those days hinds were getting £6 a week, and he got £20 in four days, but by Jove, he'd done the work.'

Another advantage of the horse and cart is that the amount of damage it does to the land is relatively small, whereas tractors towing huge muckspreaders can leave deep ruts. It also means that John and David can get the muck out most days in the winter. Tractors, on the whole, are unable to do so.

'We muck about 20 acres a year by hand,' says John. 'I was always brought up in the belief that you should muck a field every third year, but we probably don't have enough to do that.' He adds, 'We don't use a lot of nitrogen. Horse-drawn implements can't really cope with crops of grass which have had heavy doses of nitrogen because they just grow too thick.'

For family and friends living close to Sillywrea, the fact that the manure is shifted by hand is an advantage. It doesn't take David too long to load up a cart with muck dug out of a hemmel and deliver it to their gardens in time for the spring. Quite a few rhubarb patches in the vicinity of Sillywrea can be said to benefit from this seasonal boost!

The Saddler

It's an incongruous sight: clasping a huge horse's collar half the size of himself, a short, thickset man in flat cap and tweed jacket picks his way through the cars parked along the town's main street. It's a bit of a collision of cultures: most of the owners of these cars wouldn't recognise the piece of agricultural history John Dodd is carrying, just as he would never dream of listening to the music they play on their cars' hi-fi systems.

It's late November. John has travelled 45 miles through countryside bathed in low winter sunlight to visit Jobsons' saddlers shop in Alnwick. His walk through the market town, home of the Percy family and Earls of Northumberland since the 14th century, has taken him past Farmers Folly, a 75-foot-high column with a lion on top. It tells a tale that brings a wry smile to the face of the hardy Pennine farmer. In 1816 the Duke of Northumberland reduced his tenant farmers' rents by a quarter after the hardships of the Napoleonic Wars. In gratitude, the tenants commissioned the column to be built in their landlord's honour. The duke, assuming that if his tenants could afford to pay for a monument they could afford to pay higher rents, promptly put them up again. 'No wonder they call it a folly!' John laughs.

A figure of a horse's head complete with bridle juts into the street over the entrance to the saddlers shop in Bondgate Within. John pushes the door open and walks in. On display is everything for the lover of the great outdoors: walking sticks, Wellingtons, fishing gear, bridles and reins, caps and water-proofs. Steps at the back of the shop lead upstairs to a room in the centre of which stands a large work table covered with pieces of leather.

'Now then,' says John. 'I'm here to bother you again.'

One of the last horsemen in England has come to meet one of the last master saddlers. His name is John Bailey.

Jobsons have been going for more than 100 years, and the workshop hasn't changed much in that time. It has electric light, but the mantles from the gas lighting still stick out of the walls. John joined the firm at the age of 16, served a seven-year apprenticeship with Cyril and Leslie Jobson and their saddler Stuart Watson, and has been there ever since. 'They were hard taskmasters,' he says. 'They showed you how to do a job properly. And if you got it wrong you were made to take it to pieces and do it again, which is the only real way to learn.' John is 42. The men who taught him have retired and he's one of only 11 master saddlers left in the country. Some claim that many of the old saddlers were the architects of their own demise. They were perfectionists, but the harness they made was so good it lasted too long.

John hefts the Clydesdale collar onto the work table and he and John Bailey launch into a conversation about leather and cloth, stuffing and stitching. From hooks on the walls hang bridles and straps in varying stages of repair. Everything is done properly at Jobsons'. But it can take time.

'Jobsons' have that much work on, things can be there for years before they get round to mending them,' says John. 'But they are high-class saddlers. They have a name to keep up, so whenever I have something I want a really good job made of, it goes to Jobsons'. You just have to be patient. You know it'll get fixed sooner or later.'

The horse collar John has brought with him is probably 70 years old. The leather is good, but the stuffing is rotten and the checked cloth lining has perished. 'Everyday harness we just patch up ourselves, but collars are a job on their own,' John explains. 'You must have a collar right or it will skin the horse's shoulders. It's a very skilled job, collar-making.'

Collars, designed to spread the load evenly across a horse's shoulders rather than on its neck and windpipe, are a comparatively recent innovation. Before they were invented, horses were fitted with broad leather breastplates for pulling, but these devices often hampered their breathing. With the development of the collar, horses came into their own.

Ideally, a horse collar should be packed with rye straw, but very few farmers grow rye these days. The saddler tells John he's heard of a farmer in Scotland who's planning to grow the crop with the aim of supplying saddlers with the straw. Wheat straw is a possibility, but unless you can go with a scythe and cut a small area yourself, as John has done in the past, it's difficult to get straw which is the right length – combine harvesters chop it too short.

John can remember when some collars were packed with sheep's wool. Would that be the answer? John Bailey shakes his head. 'Rye straw, if properly dried, won't shrink, whereas wool can shrink and go into a ball.'

Collar designs, like the design of many items in agriculture in the days before standardisation, varied from region to region. Most of the heavy horse collars that Jobsons' repair are the 'high-top' collars which were popular in Scotland and the Border counties.

It's not just repairs that keeps John Bailey so busy. He's just spent seven weeks making a full set of 'show' harness for a Welsh Cob to wear on special occasions. It's workmanship of the highest order: saddle, collar, blinkers, breeching and traces – all hand-stitched in black patent leather with yellow trims and gleaming with a myriad of brass buckles. It set the owner back £4,750, but it is a work of art.

'Saddle-making is very dear now,' says John Dodd. 'Mending a collar can be expensive. Hopefully it will last a lifetime, but some of our harness, it's out every day. When we're mucking byres in terrible weather, it gets wet and it doesn't always get properly dried.'

For new jobs like the Welsh Cob harness,

and for heavy horse equipment like John Dodd's, John Bailey relies on his 1909 reference book, *The Harness and Saddle Maker's Guide*, which contains all the right measurements for harness produced a century ago. 'Without that,' he admits, 'I'd be lost.'

The saddler's collection of specialist tools is his chief asset. The leather comes in great pieces of hide measuring 60 inches by 90 inches and is cut out with a 'plough' knife, shaped with a half-moon knife and pared with a 'skiver'. Awls are used for making stitching holes. John Bailey makes the thread by hand, taking hemp from bobbins and twisting it to achieve the thickness he wants, using wax to keep it together. Twine like this is flexible and doesn't cut the leather, and yet is extremely durable.

The other John is preparing to take his leave. 'Right,' he says, glancing at the collar he's brought. 'Just do the best you can with it.'

The saddler says: 'Well, if I patch it right you'll get another 15 to 20 years out of it.'

John laughs. 'It'll see me out then.'

'Aye,' says the saddler. 'And me as well.'

Lifting Turnips

Turnips are an essential ingredient of the sheep's diet at Sillywrea during winter and spring. Some are left in the ground to be grazed by the animals, but a large number are harvested and stored. These bulky root crops contain a high percentage of water and are vulnerable to hard frosts, so they are piled up in clamps (heaps) in a field close to the farm for easy access during the winter. Insulation against the cold weather usually comes from a covering of soil topped with layers of straw, but sometimes John uses a different cover: dried bracken weighed down with rough muck to stop the winds blowing it away. It's another throwback to the days when straw was more highly valued as a by-product of the harvest than it is today. Bracken, which grew on many farms, was a free alternative source of bedding for animals, as well as providing thick covering for heaps of root crops like turnips and potatoes.

To see John walking out to cut bracken with a scythe is another rural sight which once was common but which has now faded into the mists of time. Perhaps its disappearance has come about because bracken has a bad name nowadays; it's poisonous when it's a young plant, and its invasive colonisation of much hill ground has deprived farms of huge areas of good grazing land. But at Sillywrea, it's still regarded as a useful bonus.

John says: 'There's a big clump of bracken on a patch of waste land near the wood on one side of the farm, and in the early autumn I just take the scythe and mow it. I let it dry, and then one of us goes with the horse and cart and fetches it in. For covering a heap of turnips it's as good as straw.'

Harvesting turnips by hand is a chore remembered with a feeling of dread by many elderly farm labourers. Often carried out in the chilly days of late autumn and early winter, it was one of the toughest jobs of all. The part of the crop which is above the ground – the neck and leaves – is known as the 'shaw' in the north of England and Scotland, and shawing turnips was backbreaking torture for the men and women who did it. Bending over the rows of turnips they grasped them by the necks with their left hand, hacked off the roots and then severed the head from the neck, using a long-handled knife with a hook on the end, called a shawing (or turnip) hook. All this was done in one quick, fluid movement, because the labourers were expected to work fast. As a result, most of them bore scars on their hands. Fingers nicked by turnip hooks were an occupational hazard.

As the labourers worked their way through the crop, the tops and the turnips flew into separate heaps a few yards apart. The usual practice was to pull two rows and put the tops and turnips to the right, and then pull another two rows and put the tops and turnips to the left. There was logic to this way of working. It allowed a horse and cart to be driven up the middle for the turnips to be loaded and carted from the field. Here, too, employers didn't want their workers to waste any time. They were expected to develop a technique of picking up the turnips and throwing them as rapidly as they could into the cart with barely a glance at what they were doing. 'If you had two turnips in your hands, two in the air and two hitting the floor of the cart – all at the same time – they reckoned you were doing the job right,' says John. 'Mind, that took some keeping up. We liked to just go nice and steady. Pulling turnips by hand, we reckoned on doing eight cartloads a day.'

On most farms the tops were loaded with graipes into carts and taken away to be fed to sheep. Nothing had to be wasted.

As the winter wore on, the tops of the turnips died back and there was nothing for a farm worker to grab. Moreover, when it was frosty many of the turnips were stuck fast in the soil. That's when the turnip knife came fully into its own. The hook on the tip was used to hoick the turnips out of the ground before the blade was used to cut off the roots.

At Sillywrea, the turnips are still occasionally pulled by hand. But more often than not, John uses a mechanical lifter made by the Wiltshire company, Parmiter. It's at least 50 years old. Pulled by a single horse, the machine runs on four small wheels mounted on adjustable bars which determine its depth. The operator controls it by holding the two stilts (handles) at the back. The lifter is fitted with two blades at the front of the frame, which slice the tops of the turnips off, and a pan at the rear which cuts the turnips off at the roots. In good conditions, it makes neat work of lifting and trimming the turnips, but when the land is heavy after showers of rain, the small wheels tend to clog up.

Nevertheless, it's one of John's favourite machines. 'I'd never seen a horse-drawn turnip lifter before but I'd heard about them and I was determined to get one,' he grins. 'We went to a farm sale in Westmorland where it was advertised at and as soon as it came up I went after it. The price wasn't really that bad. I think it cost £120 which was a bit more than I'd have preferred to pay, but it's proved to be extremely good value. In terms of the time it's saved, the money was well spent. You could lift four or five acres of turnips a day if you wanted to, but we just harvest as much as we can lead in in a day with a horse and cart.'

Nor do they bend and pick up the turnips by hand. 'We use hay forks,' says John. 'In the old days it was completely forbidden because it left two prick holes in the turnip, but we find it doesn't seem to affect them a great deal, so we stick to forks.'

Fattening Geese

Fattening a few geese for Christmas is a tradition that lingers on at Sillywrea. Half a dozen six-week-old goslings arrive at the farm in July and spend the next six months putting on weight so that they can be ready for the festive season. The birds are fed scraps from the kitchen and waste corn from the granary. During the day they graze the orchard. 'I like a goose,' John says. 'We generally have one at the New Year.' Country dwellers, brought up close to the land, have always taken a lively interest in what ends up on their table.

The family also used to rear about 20 turkeys every year. But not any longer. 'Too much work,' John says. 'Too little profit. Selling them is just like selling sheep – one year you have a good do, next year you can't give them away. One Christmas we were all laid up with the flu, but we had to keep going because people were relying on us for their turkeys. So after that we stopped bothering with them.'

In the 19th century, the demand for turkeys and geese for the Christmas table was so strong that farmers used to drive flocks of birds huge distances to markets in cities like London. To protect their webbed feet over the long journeys, they often dipped them in tar or swaddled them in leather or sacking.

Winter Feeding

If there's ice in November to bear a duck
The rest of the winter will be clarts and
    muck

It's a chilly Sunday in December. The clarts (muddy patches) have frozen over and the farm is enveloped in snow. Icicles hang in rows from the gutters. The horses' water troughs are solid. Winter has come with a vengeance to Sillywrea.

John and David don't normally work on Sundays. They only do essential things. 'Six days shalt thou labour and on the seventh shalt thou rest,' says John. 'When I was a laddie you very rarely saw anyone working on a Sunday. But the war changed all that. There was more tillage and more crops to win. People worked all the time. They had the theory that if the soldiers had to fight on a Sunday then the farmers should work on Sundays too.

'We still don't work on Sundays apart from when it's necessary, but I must admit the last five years we have worked among the hay or harvest on a Sunday if it's ready to get.'

When there's snow on the ground, there's only one way for David and John to get hay to cattle in a distant field – by horsedrawn sledge. They've got two to choose from. One they made themselves out of heavy planks with home-made metal runners to protect the wood. The other they spotted in an advert in the local paper.

'It was a real hay sledge, properly made years ago by a joiner and a blacksmith. It had been used until the 1970s by a man with a small dairy farm. When the snow came he'd use it to take the milk churns along to the end of the farm lane to be collected by the milk wagon. Since those days it had been lying hidden at the back of a hayshed and he'd come across it one day and decided to get rid of it.'

John and David spent several evenings

renovating the sledge and giving it a new lick of paint. They removed the 'coop' (body) from a derelict farm cart and fixed it onto the sledge to increase its carrying capacity. Shafts were fitted to the front.

On this particular occasion, they opt for the home-made model. Out of the stable comes Davey wearing chain harness. The chains are hooked to a swingletree attached to the front of the sledge. 'We just cobbled the sledge up ourselves,' John says. 'It's not a sophisticated thing, but it's useful, come snowy weather.'

It's bright and cold. David's wearing mittens to protect his hands from the frozen reins. John has a cap with earmuffs. But he doesn't mind the snow and frost: 'I like this kind of weather, it's better than rain or clarts.'

They set off towards the fell. Silence hangs over the landscape. The sound of the horse's hooves is muffled. The sledge, gliding in its steel runners, is loaded with bales of hay. John sits up top, happy to have a ride as it swishes over the wintry fields. For safety's sake, they pick a level route. A sledge is a fine way to transport feed in the snow, but without any form of brake, it can be a liability when it's heading downhill because it can slide into the horse's fetlocks. In fact, people used to take chains with them to slip under the runners so as to slow down a farm sledge when it was in danger of running away.

The cattle are Simmental cows and calves. Along with the other continental beef breeds – Charolais, Limousin, Blonde d'Aquitaine and Belgian Blue – these Swiss cattle have been popular in Britain for about three decades. They were due to go inside buildings at the farm, but the weather's been dry enough for them to remain outside. The men leave them a heap of sweet-smelling hay.

'On a nice, frosty morning like this the cattle are taking no harm being out on the fell. It's when it comes clashy, windy weather that they suffer. And the land takes as much harm as the cattle, because they plunge it so much. That's when we'll bring them in. Land's too scarce and too dear these days for it to be wasted like that.'

The cattle fed, the men turn for home. They have to traverse three snow-covered fields to reach the farm. From a distance, it's an almost elemental sight: the horse-drawn sledge with one man sitting on it and the other walking alongside. Figures etched black against the dazzlingly white snow.

'Aye,' says John: 'There'll not be many sledges left on working farms. Hill farms used to yoke a shepherd's pony onto a sledge to take some hay to outlying sheep. But most of them have got farm bikes now. We're probably among the last.'

New Year's Eve

It's half past eleven on 31 December and in the village of Allendale in Northumberland revellers are starting to gather in the square to welcome in the New Year in the traditional style. Among the crowd are John, Maggie, David and Richard. They've travelled the three miles from Sillywrea to watch. Frances would have liked to come, but she's at home looking after her aged granny. 'We don't go every year,' says David, 'but we thought Richard was old enough now to see the New Year in, and as it's a local custom we thought it would be an excellent idea for him.'

Allendale is a special place to wave good-bye to the old year. For as long as anyone can remember, the people of the village have staged a flamboyant procession on New Year's Eve. Forty-five men from the area, 'Guisers' disguised in a variety of costumes, carry barrels of blazing tar round the streets before flinging them under a huge bonfire as the church clock strikes midnight. Led by the Braes of Allen silver band, the crowd then launch into 'Auld Lang Syne'.

Whether the 'Tar Barls' ceremony has its origins in pagan times isn't known for certain, but it's likely to have stemmed from then. Word handed down from one generation to the next suggests that, in times gone by, villagers went into each other's houses with blazing torches to frighten out the spirits of the old year and clear the way for the spirits of the new. In order to escape retribution from the sprits they'd banished, they wore disguises.

Preparations for the event start some weeks before, with the arrival in Allendale of the barrels. Originally they were proper tar barrels, but a shortage of those has forced the fire festival committee to look elsewhere. Now they use 40-gallon whisky barrels or herring barrels. The ends are cut off to form the wooden dishes the Guisers carry. They're filled with shavings and kindling before being doused with paraffin, ready to be set alight as the procession is about to get under way.

On the Saturday before New Year's Eve the fire festival committee meet in Allendale market place to build the bonfire. Forming the base and allowing a good draught to get under the heap of dried larch branches are the middles of the barrels. They provide a solid, flammable base.

Unlike Guy Fawkes Night, no figure is perched on top of the heap.

Only people born and bred in the Allen Valley may carry a barrel. They joke that when a child is born in Allendale they lift it up by the ankles and drop it on the floor to make sure it has a flat head. That way it'll be fit to carry a barrel when it grows up!

Over the years Guisers have had to cope with all kinds of conditions: rain, sleet, frost and snow. The worst is wind, because it fans the flaming barrels so that they singe people's hair and send showers of sparks up into the night air. But the committee's rules are strict: if you drop your barrel you're not allowed to carry one the following year. The barrels are heavy and only one woman has ever been permitted to carry one. She was Vesta Peart, and she was only allowed to take part because she had made many of the costumes.

'I've only been a few times in my life,' says John, 'but it's a friendly occasion. It's all in good spirit. It's nice to see the New Year in. They often say farmers are only happy when they're complaining. But it's also true that they're great optimists. You always hope next year is going to be better.'

The Ploughman

At 1.45 p.m. on 20 January 1998 John Dodd stood in the chilly vastness of Holy Trinity Church at Cambo in Northumberland, waiting for a funeral service to begin. He was there with a handful of other mourners to pay their respects to Tom Forster, someone who truly was a 'friend of the earth'. As the congregation rose to sing 'The Lord is My Shepherd' John looked at the coffin lying on trestles in front of the altar. The flowers on it were arranged to form a distinctive shape: the pointed wedge of a ploughshare. It was a fitting way to honour the man who'd been one of Britain's greatest ploughmen.

Tom Forster was born in a cottage at Bascoe Dyke near Alnstable in the old county of Cumberland on 17 July 1906. His father was a labourer on the farm, a typical Eden Valley holding with cattle and sheep and a stable of horses. This was the zenith in the fortunes of heavy horses. The annual count of farm animals for 1906 reported that there were 22,000 horses doing agricultural work on Cumberland's farms, with half as many again involved in non-agricultural work. In the early years of the 20th century, horses ruled the farms.

The Forsters, like all farm workers, were poor. Tom's father was paid 16 shillings and 9 pence (about 84p) for a 58-hour week. The tied cottage came with the job. The family could have all the firewood they wanted and there was a plot to grow some vegetables. But there wasn't much scope for luxuries.

Tom's earliest memory was a striking one. He could remember as a tiny child walking along the broad, empty shore of the Solway Firth. He was dragging a piece of driftwood behind him. As he watched the sand curve from the stick and fall in even lines, like furrows rippling from a plough, he knew instinctively what he wanted to be. In the distance he could hear his mother: 'Tom! Tom!' But he was oblivious to her calls. He was only four, but the die was cast. He would grow up and become a ploughman.

All his life Tom would hark back to that moment.

When he was five his family moved to

work on a farm near Hexham in Northumberland. Tom was supposed to go to the village school but for a boy brought up with horses there were other more pressing attractions. If he saw someone ploughing in the fields on the way to school he'd skip classes and follow the furrow. He could read and write, but only just. By the time he'd reached 12, he was already on a farm working his way up to becoming a ploughman.

In Cambo Church, John joined in as the congregation sang:

We plough the fields and scatter
The good seed on the land...

Then the service was over and the coffin had gone.

Standing among other mourners in the snowbound churchyard, John recalled how his friendship with Tom had begun in early autumn 25 years before. 'There was a knock at the door one Sunday evening and standing on the step was this tall man smoking a pipe. He'd come to ask if he could borrow some horses to use at the local ploughing matches. He'd won so many prizes with tractors that he'd decided to go back to his first love. He wanted to plough with horses again. I had a brother-in-law who managed a farm in the Cambo district and he used to tell me about this grand ploughman, Tom Forster, and how there was nothing he didn't know about farms in Northumberland. So that night when he came for a loan of the horses, well, for all I didn't know him, I was happy to help him. I'd heard such a lot about him.'

Tom's early years in farming were tough. Employment wasn't easy to find. In spring and autumn, women (known as servant girls) and male farm workers ('servant lads' or 'hinds') lined up at hiring fairs in market towns and waited for work. The demeaning nature of such job-seeking forced many men to go about it surreptitiously. In some places, a straw in the corner of the mouth or sticking out of a cap was the only sign that a hind was for hire. Potential employers walked up and down eyeing the men, assessing their strength, questioning them. How old were they? Were they married? Where had they worked previously? What experience did they have? A young lad, who had never worked on a farm before, wasn't in a very strong bargaining position, because farmers knew they'd be spending a lot of their time teaching him. But as men worked their way up, they could ask for bigger wages.

There was a lot of haggling over money. Once a deal was done, palms were struck and the worker would receive a shilling to show his employer meant business. This was called 'earnest money' in some districts. Naturally, it was deducted from the man's eventual pay. In the 1920s a 'hind' was supposed to be paid £3 for three months, in arrears. Often it was less. Admittedly, he got his board and lodging as well. But that varied. Some farms fed their men well; others kept them going on porridge, broth, and bread and cheese. A treat was herring cooked on top of potatoes. Tom used to say: 'Like damned slaves, that's what we were. Damned slaves. Some farmers treated their dogs better than their men.'

At one farm he worked on, his master was renowned for having a mean streak. Although bedridden from arthritis, the old man would watch his men at work in the field in front of the house through a mirror hanging on the bedroom wall. At one point the field vanished from view behind a railway embankment. The farmer would take his watch and time how long it took horse and man to reappear. 'If you'd stopped to light your pipe he'd play war,' Tom remembered. 'That was the kind of man he was.' On one notorious occasion, the farmer took exception to the way a field had been prepared for sowing turnips. Tom had planned the ploughing wrongly, he claimed. There were too many 'butts' (short rows), he said. It looked untidy Tom was ordered to level off the field and start again.

There was a 20-year difference in their ages, but the friendship between John and Tom grew. They shared a love of the land and a passion for horses. And although John is a farmer and Tom had been a labourer, there was mutual respect. Both men agreed that modern farming methods put too much pressure on the land. 'Farmers these days,' Tom would growl, unable to hide his disgust. 'They're in too much of a damned hurry.'

What they really enjoyed was swapping tales about farming in the hard times before the Second World War. John would recall a farm where a young woman was employed to work in the farm house, as many were in those days. Kitchen chores included baking. The woman was told to make two kinds of apple pie: one with the soft flesh of cooking apples (for the family), the other with the sour peelings (for the farm staff). Next day the farmer's wife was visited by friends. Unable to tell which was which, the servant woman mistakenly produced the pie with the peelings. It was a genuine error, but next day she was sacked. 'They were hard times, true enough,' John says.

On many farms in the years between the First and Second World Wars life for farm labourers like Tom was much as it had been in the latter years of the 19th century. Conditions were spartan. Farm lads lived in the farm house, three or four to a room, frequently having to share a bed. Many slept in their work clothes, because their spare clothes were often away being washed, in most cases by a farm worker's wife under an arrangement that she would be paid when the lad got his pay at the end of his six months.

It was murky in the bedroom. There was no electricity. Light came from a candle or a paraffin lamp, but it was usually a struggle to read. Every bed had a chamber pot under it, because the earth closet (toilet) was outside across the yard. Toilet paper was cut-out squares of newspaper threaded on a string – one of the servant girl's many chores.

The workers' bedroom would generally be above the kitchen, where a great iron range blazed all night. So at least there was some vestigial warmth. But little was done to integrate the workers into the life of the farmer and his family. In many cases there was a ladder leading from a trapdoor in the lads' bedroom to the back kitchen, whose door led to the yard, so that the men (and their dirty boots) were kept out of the way as much as possible.

At one farm he worked at, Tom remembered that the farmer would start the day by banging on the floor of the workers' room with a broom handle from below and yelling at them to get up. At 5.30 in the morning. Seizing their caps and coats they would tumble down the ladder and pull on their boots before stumbling to the stable to muck out and feed their horses. The head horseman would shout which harness the horses should be fitted with, depending on what job the farmer had decided on for the day.

Summoned by a bell, the lads would return to the farm house at quarter to seven to bolt down their breakfast. The food was plain but wholesome – home-cured bacon, home-baked bread and tea. But there was no time for lingering. 'Double your bread,' one hard-faced farmer's wife once told a friend of Tom's. 'You'll eat it faster that way.' Breakfast over, the men returned to the stable to plait their horses' tails in readiness for the day's work before leaving for the fields on the stroke of seven. At noon, workers and horses would come back to the farm to water and rest the horses, and after lunch they would resume their work in the fields, finishing at five o'clock – if there was enough light to stay out that long. The day's final task would be to remove the harness in the stable, hang it up, groom the horses and feed them. Work would be finished by 7 p.m.

On some farms, the horsemen didn't come home for dinner but remained in the field. While their horses munched their feed from large nosebags, the men sat propped against a hedge wolfing down their 'bait' (packed meal). Typical fare would be slices of bread-and-dripping and a bottle of tea wrapped in an old sock to keep it lukewarm.

Saturdays might have been a day off for people in other occupations, but not on farms. Farm workers were expected to work Saturdays, but they were given Sundays off in most places.

In those days there was a strict hierarchy among farm workers. At the top was the head horseman, and it was an unwritten rule that his pair of horses should be harnessed first and be first out of the stable in the morning and first back into the stable at night. At the kitchen table, when meals were served to the workers, it was the same pecking order. The head horseman helped himself first, followed by the other men in descending order of experience.

In *Akenfield*, Ronald Blythe's portrait of an English village (published in 1969), a retired farm worker recalls his days on a large farm teeming with heavy horses during the 1920s:

The head horseman was the 'lord' – and that's what he was, lord of all the horses. The place ran like clockwork. All the harnessing was done in strict order, first this, then that. The ploughing teams left and returned to the stable yards according to the rank of the ploughman. If you happened to get back before someone senior to you, you just had to wait in the lane until he arrived.

The horses were friends and loved like men. Some men would do more for a horse than they would for a wife. The ploughmen talked softly to their teams all day long and you could see the horses listening. Although the teams ploughed 20 yards apart the men didn't talk to each other, except sometimes they sang. Each man ploughed in his own fashion and with his own mark. It looked all the same if you didn't know about ploughing but a farmer could walk on a field ploughed by 10 different teams and tell which bit was ploughed by which. Sometimes he would pay a penny an acre extra for perfect ploughing. Or he would make a deal with the ploughman – free rent for good work. That could mean £5 a year. The men worked perfectly to get this, but they also worked perfectly because it was their work. It belonged to them.

The horsemen were the big men on the farm. They kept in with each other and had secrets. They whispered lot. If someone who wasn't a ploughman came upon them talking, they'd soon change the conversation!

This was the world that Tom ached to inhabit. His only ambition was to be head horseman. At the age of 19 he achieved it. He always said he was the youngest man to do so – at any rate in the district where he worked.

In 1940, after 15 years of moving from farm to farm, Tom's fortunes changed. He was taken on as ploughman by Sir Charles Trevelyan, of Wallington Hall in Northumberland. By this time, pay was fixed by county agricultural committees. Tom's wage was £3 a week. 'I well remember my first day at Wallington,' he would say, looking back in his later years. 'October the 22nd. A hell of a wet day. But, mind, November that year was a lovely month and we got a lot done on the land.' Tom had an extraordinary memory for the weather. He could remember bad years, when farmers were still cutting corn in November, and good years when they finished making hay as early as June.

He settled with his wife Mary in a house in the courtyard of Wallington Hall and enjoyed a secure life at last. Horses gave way to tractors as the wartime drive towards producing more food accelerated. And as the years went by, Tom, encouraged by his employer, entered tractor ploughing competitions all over England. The results were there to see on the walls of his workshop at Wallington. They were papered with prize tickets.

Tom enjoyed a good relationship with Sir Charles Trevelyan. The landowner's life had been an unusual one. Converted from Liberalism to Socialism during the First World War, he stood for Parliament as a Labour candidate in Newcastle Central, won the seat and became President of the Board of Education in the first Labour Government in 1924. Socially, the gulf between him and Tom was huge, but the two men respected one another.

The Wallington estate covered 13,000 acres of Northumberland countryside. Sir Charles was later to give it all away to the National Trust but in the 1940s he took an active interest in running the estate, which included the Home Farm, where Tom was employed. At harvest time, Tom would drive a tractor and binder round a field of ripened barley, with Sir Charles, a crack shot, riding on the back and picking off the rabbits as they emerged from the stubble. But when it came to building stacks with sheaves of corn, Tom would banish his boss from the stackyard. 'He wanted to help,' he'd say. 'But he just got in the way. Building a stack is a skilled job and he was just a darned nuisance.' Sir Charles, then in his seventies, meekly accepted his worker's orders.

At 65, Tom retired from farm work. But instead of putting his feet up he bought a tractor and began a new career hiring himself out as a freelance ploughing contractor. When his wife Mary died, he was heartbroken. They had no children. Tom grieved deeply. He said it was the work that helped him through. He carried on ploughing – and he was still doing it at the age of 90. He knew every field in the district, and he knew how they should be ploughed. 'There are a lot of different soils and a lot of different shapes of fields,' he would say. 'You've got stony fields and fields with lovely sandy soil. And you've sloping fields. You have to decide whether to plough across them or up and down. It's all a question of having your plough set right. If you have, you can just about put your hands in your pockets and leave the tractor to it.' Tom didn't charge an exorbitant amount for his work, and if farmers were slow in paying he didn't chase them. He was too easy-going for his own good.

John Dodd and Tom continued to see each other as the years went by. Tom would come to Sillywrea for Christmas dinner, full of gossip about farms being bought and sold and farming families' comings and goings. And when John could find time, he would accompany his friend to ploughing matches in the northern counties, marvelling at how the older man had never lost his ability to control a pair of horses and plough the perfect furrow. John's Clydesdales weren't accustomed to ploughing matches watched by crowds of people. Strange sounds, like the roar of steam-driven threshers, which are often part of the attraction at such events, might easily have unnerved the horses. But in Tom's care they went quietly about their work. There was something timeless about the way he'd pick up the reins, spit on the palms of his hands, call 'Gee up!' and send horses and plough on their unerring straight path.

'Why do I keep going?' Tom used to say. 'For the love of the plough, that's why. When you're ploughing with horses and the plough's set right, you can hear the plough singing in the soil and the horses are just sailing. Man, that's a great feeling.'

Tom may be here no more, but John has something tangible to remember him by. One day, when he was in his eighties, Tom was ploughing close to the edge of a field when his shining tractor plough became entangled with something lurking in the hedge. Ironically, it was an old horse plough, left to rust more than 60 years ago. Gingerly, Tom freed the old implement from the brambles and with the farmer's blessing, took it home to 'fettle up' – restore it to its former glory.

Several years before his death he gave that plough to his friend and it's now John's pride and joy. 'That plough's one of the best we've got. Every time we get it out I think of Tom,' John says fondly. 'He was a great countryman and a grand chap. I'm glad I got to know him.'

Epilogue

Asked how he would like to be remembered, John Dodd replies: 'As a son of the soil, one who loved the land.' Like his daughter Frances, John has often felt inspired to put down his thoughts in poetry.

The following verses were composed as he walked up and down behind the plough one winter's day. They're a tribute to his own lifelong hero, ploughman Tommy Heslop. But the words could equally apply to John himself.

Up and down the fertile sod
The strong and steady horses plod
With nodding heads and tight-drawn
  chains
Guided with light hand on reins.

The ploughman with his steady gait
Guides the plough so true and straight
And as he walks with measured stride
Doing his work with love and pride
Not a dull and humble ploughman

But a proud and happy yeoman.

And when he works in sun and rain
He thinks of most things with fertile brain
Not thoughts guided by what others say
But thoughts inspired by working close to
  God each day

As he does each task in season
His life unfolds with rhyme and reason
Only the ignorant think his work is dull
His joy: the singing lark and wheeling gull
The fallow greening with the sprouting
  corn
The mists in hollows on a summer's morn.

The joy of growing roots in straight and
  weed-free rows
Or well-built stacks safe thatched from
  winter snows
The power of office he would never
  treasure
A prize for well-fed beast or straight-drawn
  plough his harmless pleasure.

He'll work with little rest or sleep
To save the lambs and tend the sheep
He'll toil long hours to save the hay
But keeps for rest the Sabbath day.

And as he tends his fields, the hoof, the
  horn
He thinks: Oh, who is man that he should
  mourn?
For man like grass is gone tomorrow
To misuse God's land a greater sorrow.

If God gave life, as sure He must
Then God gave land a sacred trust
And when the yeoman's run this earthly
  race
And stands before his Maker face to face
Should he be asked, What have you done?
And have you reached some height of
  fame?
Then he can answer without shame:
I've spent my life in honest toil
Caring for my farm and soil.

Maybe in that final Judgement Day
The Maker of the world will smile and say
Oh good and faithful servant thee
You've toiled with nature and you've
  worked with Me.

The publishers hope that this book has given you enjoyable reading. Large Print Books are especially designed to be as easy to see and hold as possible. If you wish a complete list of our books please ask at your local library or write directly to:

Magna Large Print Books
Magna House, Long Preston,
Skipton, North Yorkshire.
BD23 4ND

This Large Print Book, for people
who cannot read normal print,
is published under the auspices of

THE ULVERSCROFT FOUNDATION

... we hope you have enjoyed this book.
Please think for a moment about those
who have worse eyesight than you ...
and are unable to even read or enjoy
Large Print without great difficulty.

You can help them by sending a
donation, large or small, to:

**The Ulverscroft Foundation,
1, The Green, Bradgate Road,
Anstey, Leicestershire, LE7 7FU,
England.**
or request a copy of our brochure for
more details.

The Foundation will use all donations
to assist those people who are visually
impaired and need special attention
with medical research, diagnosis
and treatment.

Thank you very much for your help.